Writing Your Life Story

Also by Michael Legat

Novels
MARIO'S VINEYARD
THE SILVER FOUNTAIN
THE SHAPIRO DIAMOND
THE SILK MAKER
THE CAST IRON MAN

Non-fiction
DEAR AUTHOR . . .
AN AUTHOR'S GUIDE TO PUBLISHING
WRITING FOR PLEASURE AND PROFIT
THE NUTS AND BOLTS OF WRITING
PLOTTING THE NOVEL
HOW TO WRITE HISTORICAL NOVELS
NON-FICTION BOOKS: An Author's Guide
AN AUTHOR'S GUIDE TO LITERARY AGENTS
UNDERSTANDING PUBLISHERS' CONTRACTS
THE WRITER'S RIGHTS
REVISION: An Author's Guide
THE ILLUSTRATED DICTIONARY OF WESTERN LITERATURE
PUTTING ON A PLAY
WE BEHELD HIS GLORY

Writing Your Life Story

MICHAEL LEGAT

ROBERT HALE · LONDON

First published in Great Britain 1999

ISBN 0 7090 6398 9

Robert Hale Limited
Clerkenwell House
Clerkenwell Green
London EC1R 0HT

2 4 6 8 10 9 7 5 3 1

Typeset by
Derek Doyle & Associates, Mold, Flintshire.
Printed in Great Britain by
St Edmundsbury Press Limited, Bury St Edmunds
and bound by
WBC Book Manufacturers Limited, Bridgend

Contents

1 You Really Ought to Write a Book

'You've had such an interesting life – you really ought to write a book.' Has that ever been said to you? Maybe you've heard it quite frequently. Or, even if no friend has complimented you in that way, have you thought about it off your own bat, as it were? Wherever the suggestion comes from, it is a good one, worth thinking about and acting upon.

'Everyone has a book in them,' people say, and I have often joked that in most cases the book should stay there. But don't be put off by that – I wasn't really thinking of autobiography. There is a serious thought behind the joke, but it is inspired by the fact that the book which people think they have in them is all too frequently a novel, and writing a successful novel takes a great deal of skill, and imagination, and perseverance, for it must be structured, it needs to have narrative drive, it may demand a great deal of research, it usually depends on a plot involving interesting characters and situations, and the finished article must be of a suitable length for publication; in short, it requires a talent – and not any old talent – a talent for novel-writing, with all that it entails.

Writing your autobiography is an entirely different kettle of fish. The basic structure is already there in the shape of your life (although, as we shall see later, it may be a good idea to do a little jiggling of the time sequences in order to make your story more interesting), and so are the characters and situations, and indeed all the material, and while it is an advantage to have some sort of writing ability, the skills you need are far less demanding than for fiction. You can't dispense with perseverance, because it is it going to be a disappointment to everyone, including yourself, if you give up part way through; but you have to work with a certain diligence and tenacity to succeed at just about anything in life that you want to do and which is worth doing. As for the skills, I shall do my best to show you how to develop them so as to tell your story to maximum effect.

Before moving to any kind of 'how-to' advice, let us look first at the 'when and why' of the subject.

When is a good time to write an autobiography? Some sports or pop stars produce their life stories when they have only just emerged from adolescence (or are still in the middle of it). That's fine if you really are a star and, more importantly, if there is a market for your book. Of course you can write your autobiography at any age, and although for most of us Thoreau hit the nail on the head when he said, 'How vain it is to sit down to write when you have not stood up to live,' as long as you have something to say, you can start at any time. Like now.

However, if you agree with Mr Thoreau, an ideal time might be when you have just retired from whatever has been your life's work – writing your own story might be just the job to fill those idle hours. On the other hand, if you are one of those who are so busy after retirement that you wonder how you ever found time to go to work, maybe you had better wait until your non-stop activity has slowed down a little, perhaps with advancing age. But don't leave it too long – as we become ancient, memories begin to fade. Writing your story could also help to fill the loneliness that you may feel in widowhood.

Let me repeat, however, that there are no rules on this subject. Write your life story whenever you want to. If the urge is there, it is almost certainly a good time to start, even if you are still youthful in age as well as in spirit. After all, you can write additional volumes as you get older.

As for why you should write an autobiography, there are several good reasons.

Firstly, it is a good idea because your story will be unique, and it is always worthwhile and indeed immensely rewarding to produce something which no one else on earth could duplicate. You may protest that such a concept is all very well for those whose friends are in the habit of revealing (all too frequently?) what interesting lives they have lived, but your own life has nothing really unusual about it – you have not made a million overnight, you have not saved the world from disaster, you have never been anywhere more exotic than Majorca, you have never met anyone famous, and the only honest word to describe your existence from birth until now is 'humdrum'. Don't you believe it! No one's life is devoid of interest. It may not capture headlines all over the world, or even in your local newspaper where 'Garden Party Rained Off' may be the top news-item of the week, but because human beings are all different they are endlessly fascinating. This is especially true because we all have our Seven Veils with which we conceal our real selves: we may take off one veil for acquaintances, another for close friends, and probably a couple more for our nearest and dearest, but it isn't just the Seventh Veil that we retain – that's the one that never comes off – but for most of the time the Fifth and Sixth too. We tend to be secret persons, with our private thoughts. Now, in writing an autobiography the author often feels able to reveal rather more than usual and that adds interest. The events of your life may be unexciting, but when you set forth your deeply personal view of them, your opinions, the influences on you and the circumstances in which you have found yourself, they can all be transformed into intriguing reading. So you might think of your autobiography as not just a story but as an opportunity to share your memories, whether they are happy, sad, or even bitter, and to strip off an extra veil as you do so.

It is possible to allow yourself this self-revelation because, although you write with the expectation that people will eventually read what you have written, while you are writing it there is no one to judge, to condemn or praise or argue, and there is no one to interrupt. You can get things off your chest, and put your point of view without anyone contradicting you or stopping you by saying, 'Let's change the subject.' Especially if there is something in your life about which you feel particularly bitter, you may be able to write about it far more easily than you can talk about it, and could write about it in a book more readily than in a letter, for a book, however much it is your personal testament, is somehow more detached than a letter. And by writing about your anger or your worries you will often find that the act of putting them on paper diminishes their power over you, and you can even in some cases exorcize them altogether. Obviously, this can have a beneficial, therapeutic effect. And that's a second reason for writing about your life.

A third, related reason is that you may be surprised to discover how much you find out about yourself of which you were previously unaware. Writing can release your subconscious thoughts and feelings, and almost any experienced writer will be able to tell you of moments when the writing seems to take charge, to express unexpected ideas and move in unplanned directions – it is the kind of experience that novelists refer to when they talk of their characters 'coming to life and taking over'. It is usually good to allow the writing to take over, as it were, and let the words pour out without trying to censor them. E.M. Forster spoke of the writer letting a bucket down into the subconscious, and being as surprised as anyone else by what comes up in it. Writing your autobiography can often be an exercise in self-examination – maybe it always should be – and discovering emotions which you did not know you had, and realizing the lasting effect that almost forgotten incidents have had on you, and assessing objectively your virtues and your vices – all this can be extremely instructive, and as therapeutic as getting matters off your chest. (Don't worry, by the way, if you find yourself writing things which your subconscious has turned up, but which you would prefer to stay in obscurity – you can always have second thoughts, and cut them out at a later stage.)

Looking back to your childhood and trying to examine your earliest memories in some detail can be very revealing. The influence of the first few years of our lives is of enormous importance in forming not only our characters, but, for most of us, our interests and the milieu in which we choose to make our homes and our friends. Our roots lie in our ancestry, but also very much in our childhood. If this is not so for you, and if you have broken away from your upbringing, then your story may be all the more interesting.

Fourthly (and this could be the most important reason of all), you should write your story because it will be of special interest to everyone you know, from your close family to distant relatives, from intimate friends to mere acquaintances, and especially to those of younger generations than your own. How I wish that my grandparents had written their autobiographies. I have only the sketchiest of ideas of how they lived, and know absolutely nothing about their childhood and youth, and although I could tell you quite a lot about my parents from the time when I was old enough to be really aware of them as human beings rather than just as 'Mummy' and 'Daddy', I know far too little about their earlier years. And in none of these cases am I talking about exciting information about people who were remarkable in some way or other. I would be satisfied, indeed delighted, to find little scraps of information – that my father's parents spent their honeymoon in Dunbar (or wherever it was), or that the reason for my mother spending some months in Germany, long before she met my father, was . . . well, whatever it was. Everyone to whom I talk on these lines agrees – we should all write diaries, with long entries for every day, relating not only what we did that day, but what was going on in the world, and what we thought about it, and what the price of petrol was, and what book we were reading and whether we were enjoying it, and telling of anything in the least unusual which had happened, and writing down the joke which had made us laugh so much, and so on. A diary as detailed and diverse as that could make each of us into a Pepys of our time (and you could write any rude bits in code, as he did). If you have always kept such a diary, or if the idea appeals to you and you decide to start now, more power to you, but it doesn't rule out the need for you to write an autobiography, because the diary can never take an overall view, and if you haven't kept a detailed diary in the past, but are going to start now, then you still need to cover the years when you weren't writing daily entries. Besides, you will almost certainly give up the diary after a while, because you forget or because it becomes something of a chore, but, although you will need to persevere and discipline yourself into fairly regular writing, the autobiography will make lighter demands on you than the diary would.

Fifthly, you may have something of importance which you want to say. You may feel a desire to set out your philosophy of life, or to put it in less grand terms, to tell your readers simply what life has taught you. The longer we live, the more we learn, and the more certain we become of various truths, and the less sure of others – this is wisdom, and wisdom is always worth passing on to others. Or perhaps you have a special message that you want to get across, and inserting it into an autobiography can sometimes be a more effective way of finding an audience for it than concentrating solely on whatever pet theme it might be. If, for instance, you want to tell the world that no one should ever drink wine, you could write a book about it, but far fewer of your friends would read that, whereas they might be more prepared to absorb the message if it were incorporated into your autobiography merely as a part of it. Or perhaps you want to expose an injustice, and that is the sort of material that can evoke great interest – if it is well handled.

Another possibility on the same theme is that you have, over the years, acquired a considerable knowledge of some particular subject, which you know would be of interest to a great many people, and you feel that the way to pass on your knowledge would be in an autobiographical form. It is what is sometimes known as the 'thematic' autobiography, and a book of that sort stands a very good chance of being accepted for publication, and of selling well. The only question is whether, since the subject is going to be of far more importance than your own part in it, it can properly be regarded as an autobiography, rather than simply as a straightforward non-fiction book on that subject.

Sixthly, writing is a creative act, and that applies whether what you write is fiction or fact. If you complete your autobiography, or even if you get only half way through it, the sense of achievement as you look at the pile of paper will be enhanced by the fact that you have created it. You can feel jolly pleased with yourself when you finish making a dress or painting the garage door, but you didn't make the material of the dress and you almost certainly worked from a pattern, while the door was already there, and you bought the paint and simply applied it – the creative input in either case was minimal. But your autobiography, created out of nothing but your memories (aided perhaps by various documents and other papers and photographs) will be all yours, and something to be proud of. Moreover, if you are not already aware of this, you should know that writing itself is an immensely pleasurable activity. Never believe all those published authors who tell the world that writing is 'agony'. It can certainly be hard work, demanding a great deal of care and application, but far from being agony, it's a delight, especially when you begin to hone your skills and can see that what you are putting down on paper is not only well written, but conveys exactly the shade of meaning that you intended. I will guarantee that once you really get into the swing of writing, you will resent having to stop, and will look forward to your next session. It is like most other hobbies – once you get hooked, you begin to realize that it is not just a hobby, but a craft, and that the more you practice it, the more you improve your skill, and the greater the pleasure which you will get out of it.

Seventhly, you might be considering writing an autobiography in the hope of getting it published. This is almost certainly what your friends have in mind when they tell you that you ought to write a book. It is not of course as easy as all that, and the whole subject will be discussed at some length in Chapter 10. In the meantime, let us say simply that the thought of being published is certainly a valid spur to any writer, and many autobiographies do get into print.

One poor reason for considering an autobiography is in order to make money. You will do so, of course, if you are a celebrity of some kind and your fans or people interested in your life's work will buy your book. An alternative possibility is that, even if you are not all that well known, you have something scandalous to say or are willing to reveal matters which are supposed to remain secret – one thinks of *Spycatcher*, the book which offended against the Official Secrets Act. You might also gain a substantial return from your writing if the book is of the kind which receives considerable and favourable attention in the press because of the high quality of the writing, allied to an acute observer's eye – Laurie Lee's *Cider With Rosie* is an excellent example of just such a book. What is far more likely, however, even if you succeed in getting your book commercially published, is that the rewards will not be noteworthy, and, although a few hundred pounds may be welcome, and you will also have the pleasure of seeing yourself in print, your earnings from the book will certainly not provide you with enough to live on.

However, seven reasons for writing your autobiography should be sufficient. Even if all of them do not apply to you, you ought to find enough to encourage you to start.

Two things should boost your confidence. The first is that you will be writing for like-minded people, and in saying that I am looking beyond the immediate circle of your relations and friends. If your abiding interest is in stock-car racing or reading or gardening or pop music or pigeons or, of course, in whatever work you do or did, then people who have no connection with you at all will enjoy your book, and will read it (if it is published and effectively promoted) because they share that interest. Since your interests more often than not reflect your life style, those who share them will indeed tend to be like-minded people.

The second reassurance comes from the fact that, unless you are trying to open a literary career with your autobiography, you have no need to fear any critics. If you are starting out to become a novelist or an historian or to write how-to books, you will be hoping for good reviews, and fearing those which are unfavourable. But if you are writing a one-off autobiography, the critics will not matter to you. The people for whom you are writing – primarily your friends and relations – will probably be enthusiastic (they are unlikely anyway to tell you if they find the book disappointing).

The best reason of all for writing an autobiography is quite simply that you want to do it. So get started now – except that it might be wiser to read the rest of this book first.

2 Planning

Thinking About Writing

Once you have decided to go ahead and write the story of your life you will probably want to put pen to paper (or fingers to keys) straight away, but I would suggest that you need first to stop and think. Writing is not just writing – it's thinking too, planning, shaping, deciding what you want to do and how to do it. There is a sort of joke which says that when authors are found at their desks with their eyes closed, their heads sunk upon their chests, they always deny indignantly that they are asleep, claiming instead to be thinking about their work. It is very easy to nod off when the words aren't flowing well, especially if you've had a good lunch, but in fact authors accused of dozing off are often right to feel misjudged, because they really are thinking about their writing rather than sleeping. As many professionals will tell you, books don't just write themselves – they have to be thought about, not only before the writing begins, but during it, and indeed after it. If you write a book, you need to be fully committed to it, and if you are about to embark on an autobiography, you might as well warn your nearest and dearest, especially if they have had no previous experience of a writer at work, that it will occupy a great deal of your time, and that you are going to be very much absorbed in it. (And, in order to pre-empt the funny remarks, you might explain straight away exactly what you will be doing if found apparently having a little zizz when you are supposed to be writing.)

What Approach Will You Use?

When you begin to think about writing your life story, the first question you should ask yourself is what sort of autobiography you want to write. There are many alternatives. Will your book take the form of a cradle-to-one-foot-in-the-grave account of your life, told in chronological order and endeavouring to cover all aspects of your experiences? Or will it be much more selective, perhaps dealing with your career in some detail, but neglecting the more personal side? Do you want to avoid the chronological approach, covering various crucial episodes, but not necessarily in the time sequence in which they took place, and perhaps with diversions into pen portraits of people you have known and other somewhat extraneous material, so that the result might more appropriately be called 'memoirs', rather than a full autobiography? Will you perhaps concentrate on your childhood – a number of books of that kind have been very successfully published (see pp. 123–4) – and aim to evoke a whole period rather than simply telling your own story?

One of the main options open to you is not, in fact, to write a full autobiography at all, especially if much of your life could be considered to consist of boring routine, but to concentrate on what happened in what you think of as your most exciting, adventurous experiences. This is why people write about what happened to them in wartime, or when they sailed alone around the world, or how they discovered a lost civilization or a cure for arthritis. Your story doesn't necessarily have to be as newsworthy as any of the last three, but it can be just as interesting in a less dramatic way.

For Whom Are You Writing?

This is an important question which you need to ask yourself at a very early stage. If your book is intended to be simply for your close relatives, you will probably want to concentrate on your personal life, and you will not need to explain everything about the family, because most of your readers will know all the facts, apart, of course, from events and relationships which happened before some of them were born (we are usually remarkably ignorant, as I have already observed, about family matters concerning the generations before our own). You will also be able include all those extraordinarily unfunny family jokes and little anecdotes which would be of no interest except to those who know or knew the people involved, and you can give free rein to your opinions on this, that and the other subject. On the other hand, if you are going to write for a wider audience, you will need to leave out as much as possible of the trivial material, unless it is genuinely interesting or amusing, and give only sufficient background to the main events in your story for outside readers to follow and understand what you are saying. You would, in fact, concentrate on the most important aspects of your life, and perhaps use some of the techniques which will be discussed in Chapter 4 to enhance their effect.

Writing About Yourself

A few pitfalls lie in wait for the autobiographer, and they are best avoided by thinking about them before you begin to write, so that you know they are there and can take precautions to keep out of their way.

You should not feel any embarrassment at the idea of writing mainly about yourself. Of course your autobiography will be entirely self-centred – there is no reason why it shouldn't be. Unless your self-portrait is absurdly prejudiced in your own favour, no censure can be attached to you on the grounds of your story being an ego-trip, because you are, after all, setting out to show that you have indeed lived a life worth writing about, and other people and background events need be explored in the book only to the extent that they have had a major effect on you. So don't leave yourself out because of a misplaced sense of modesty.

On the other hand, you don't want to sound pompous, or vain, or a whinger, or eaten up by jealousy or envy. You need to be careful about boastfulness, too – you may have had a remarkably successful life, but if you tell your readers of nothing but a series of triumphs, they may not only see your book as an ego-trip, but may begin to doubt your truthfulness. Be as honest as you can, and show your faults, and your misjudgements and your failures as well as the better elements in your character. Of course, if you are normally pompous, vain, a whinger, jealous, envious, and given to boasting, there may be nothing much you can do about it. But most of us have some small portion of humility in our make-up, and while complete objectivity is virtually impossible to achieve – we are too involved to see ourselves plainly – it is important to stand back, if you can, and stop yourself if you detect any signs that you are presenting your own character in a poor light. When describing some conflict with other people, try to be fair to them and present their point of view with as little of your own prejudice as possible; if you have enemies and write about them in your autobiography, give them credit for their abilities. This is not a matter of your morals as an author – it is simply true that the more balanced your picture, the more it will be to your credit.

Nevertheless, it has to be admitted that a really vicious portrayal of someone you dislike, or a hard-hitting attack on the views or behaviour of a relative or friend or business colleague can add some very welcome spice. The only problem is that you may land yourself with a libel suit (see Chapter 8).

The question of honesty, mentioned above, is an interesting one, incidentally. Most autobiographies contain a fairly large amount of fiction, partly because we mostly want to give a favourable account of ourselves, partly because of a reluctance to reveal all our innermost feelings, and partly because of faulty memory. And one of the most common causes for a lack of total honesty in the accounts we give of various incidents in the past is that, over the years, as we have told the stories on numerous occasions, they have become embroidered or 'improved' in order to make a better impact. Since there are no laws (apart from those of libel – see Chapter 8) which compel us to be totally truthful when writing an autobiography, you will naturally repeat them in your book in the form which you have developed, but it is perhaps a good thing to be aware that you have, at least slightly, distorted the truth.

You should consider too, and very seriously, the question of how much you are going to reveal of the secrets in both your personal and professional lives – how many veils you are going to strip away. The more you bare your soul, the more interesting the book will be, but of course there are always limits, even if you decide that no one is to read the book until after your death. Whether or not you strip away the protective layers behind which you, and all of us, live, you should be aware that your book may say rather more about you than you intended, and certainly more than you realize even when you read through what you have written. Although this aspect will probably be easier to deal with at revision stage when you have completed the writing of the whole book, it is yet another point to bear in mind when you are thinking about what you are going to write.

Dealing with Family, Friends and Your Business Colleagues

How widely do you intend to range in the book? Will you be including a considerable amount of material about your family, including your forebears, and your children, and your friends and your business colleagues? A series of pen portraits could be very entertaining. But how much free rein do you intend to give yourself in writing about other people and exposing not only their admirable qualities, but their various sins and wickednesses? Are you going to leave any skeletons firmly locked in the cupboard, or bare the bones to public gaze? You will have to remember that if you write too openly you may very easily upset relatives, friends and colleagues, not only by what you say about them (as a rule of thumb you can take it that anyone you know is likely to have a much thinner skin than you thought), but also, in the case of relatives, by what you say about your forebears. For example, you may find it amusing, in an indulgent way, that your grandfather was something of a Don Juan and produced a number of bastards, but your half-cousins who are descended from his indiscretions may be furious if you make the story public. Or what if a few generations back someone in your family was convicted of a serious crime? Do you tell the truth because you think it's all over and done with and there's no need to be ashamed now, or do you conceal it because you know that some of your other relations will be distressed by the disclosure, or for your own sake? Considering living relations, do you dare to say that Uncle John and Aunt Margaret are unmitigated snobs, which is true and which will amuse anyone else in the family who reads your book? You may have no qualms in divulging disagreements in the family, or the shady past of some of your ancestors, or in putting yourself in a poor light over some matter, or in telling the unpalatable truth about members of the family, but such things take on a different dimension when they are written down in cold print. You may even upset other people if you write too frankly about yourself.

The same questions will arise when you consider what you are going to say about your business colleagues. You must not write anything which might damage their careers, if they are still working, and you will have to be very circumspect about your comments in case they should reflect poorly in any way on the companies with which you and your colleagues were involved, or if you might otherwise be accused of giving away any trade secrets or other information which might be of benefit to the company's competitors.

Backgrounds

Yet another matter to be decided at this early stage is the extent to which you need to set everything that you say in your autobiography against the background of events in the outside world at the time of which you are writing. Obviously, if you were born before 1939 you will have been affected by World War II, but it is not only international upheavals of that kind which can have a major effect – your whole life may have been changed by a government decision on some matter which directly affected you, or by a natural disaster like the 1987 hurricane. While many of your readers will have a general knowledge of the major events which occurred in Britain during the period covered by your autobiography, if much of your life was spent abroad, you may need to explain what was happening where you lived, or indeed something about the physical and political geography of the background. If anything of the sort had a major part to play in your story, work out beforehand how you are going to present this material, with what amount of preparatory detail, and how it will all be dovetailed into the narrative.

What Is the Purpose of Your Book?

It may be primarily, and quite simply, that you are setting out to tell the straightforward story of your life, without using a particular angle. On the other hand, your intention might simply be to entertain, in which case you will want to concentrate on telling amusing or dramatic or particularly unusual stories, and to make your book read in many respects rather like a novel. Alternatively, do you hope to put some kind of message across? This might be to give instruction on the subject in which you have expertise, and you might then want to include a certain amount of technical detail which will be of interest principally to those with similar interests and experiences to your own; however, you will need to be careful that what you write is not all Greek to other readers who do not share your background knowledge. Or is it your intention to use the book as a vehicle for promoting and trying to convert others to your way of thinking, whether it be about your pet charity, or your political allegiance, or your belief that the earth is flat? That's fine, but how are you going to incorporate the material? You must beware of sounding as though you are preaching (which is likely to put most people off), and make your message as interesting as you can, with a few anecdotes and a touch of humour now and then to lighten the solemnity of your proselytizing. And if you find yourself carried away by your hobby-horse, so that the theme has become overwhelming, then maybe you should consider writing two books – one about yourself and one about your obsession – even if, as suggested in Chapter 1, the latter is likely to have a restricted readership.

The Dull Bits

Then you certainly need to consider how you are going to treat the duller parts of your life. We all go through periods, sometimes lasting for some years, where nothing of much interest happens – we do our routine job in a routine way, the family, if we have one, grows up, but without any special traumas, and there is very little to write about. Especially if you are using a chronological approach, you cannot simply ignore such periods, but equally you don't have to write them up at such length that you are likely to bore any reader. The answer may be to skip over such bits as quickly as possible (as a general rule, never spend more than a short paragraph on a holiday, unless something of real significance happened), or to enliven them with humour, or, indeed, you can leave them out altogether.

The Need to Plan

Each of the questions so far discussed deserves serious consideration, and it is a good idea to sort everything out in your mind at this early stage, so that you have a clear idea of what you want to do. Formulate a plan before you start the actual writing. You are not making a strait-jacket for yourself by doing so – the book is yours to do what you like with, and if, part way through writing it, you decide that the chosen approach is not after all the right one, then of course you can change it. But to know, or at least to believe you know, where you are going before you start writing will give you confidence.

As all my students over the years well know, I believe very firmly in planning as an essential part of writing, whether the work concerned is fiction or non-fiction. You may think that it would be sensible to plan a novel, so that you could sort out the plot, and the way the characters interact, and so on, because it is all imaginary. You may, however, feel that detailed planning is all very well for fiction, but is hardly necessary for an autobiography, especially if it is going to be one told chronologically from your birth onwards. However, I don't think it is as simple as that. Planning can only be helpful, especially for most beginners. If you have a plan you are far less likely to diverge from what you want to write, or to suffer from writer's block (the term which writers use when some mental hang-up prevents them from continuing with whatever they are writing at the time), and you will be able to see the vital shape and balance of your book. Writing a book is like knitting or making yourself a bookcase – if you are very experienced you may be able to produce a knitted cardigan without using a pattern, or an elegant piece of furniture without working out all the measurements first, but for most of us, the plan is a *sine qua non*.

There are all manner of matters to be considered. For instance, if you are going to begin with your birth, will you at that point describe your family in detail, including parents, grandparents, siblings, uncles and aunts and cousins, or will you leave some of them until you encounter them as you grow up? Maybe you will want to omit any mention of many of your relatives because they have played no significant or interesting part in your life, whereas perhaps business colleagues have been far more important to you. On the other hand, if you are going to write quite extensively about your family background, it is something that needs control; otherwise you might find that the material is taking up far too much space and giving an unbalanced effect to what is meant to be *your* book.

At this early stage you will need to decide not only on the relevant importance within your book of your family and the people in your business and social circles, but also on a number of other issues, as has already been suggested, such as the extent to which you will include controversial material of various kinds, or semi-instructional details relating to your main occupation, and you should look, indeed, at the whole structure of the book.

If you are not intending to follow your story chronologically, planning is even more essential. The less rigid your approach, the more likely it is that you will be using at least some of the techniques of the novelist, and if you accept that working out a pattern is needed for fiction, you will understand the point. An excellent piece of advice if you are writing a short story or a novel is to begin at or just before a moment of crisis, and in the same way you might decide to begin your autobiography at a turning-point in your life – when you began your first job, for instance, or when you scored a major success of some kind. You will still no doubt want to include at least some details of your earlier life, and these can be accommodated in what in fiction would be called flashbacks (see Chapter 4). How and when you will add in such material should be part of the planning process.

Making the Plan

To help you to make the necessary decisions, I would suggest that you start by writing down a list of all the subjects you want to cover. Just use simple words and phrases, which will be sufficient to remind you of what you were thinking of, and don't try to put them into any order – just scribble down everything which occurs to you. It might look something like the illustration (if I may call it that) on page 29. Later, when you have written down everything you can think of, it can all be sorted out. By that stage you will probably have realized what your main headings will be. As an example, you might have 'Childhood', 'Education', 'First job', 'Marriage' and thereafter '1958', '1959–62', '1963' and so on, those being the various years in which important events in your life took place, or you might have subjects and dates intermingled. Alternatively, although you still want to adhere to a chronological approach, you might find that the material seems to group itself naturally under such headings as 'Family', 'Sport', 'Financial Problems', 'Career', in which case you might decide to work from the past to the present in each of these sections.

If you mark each line with an indication (perhaps using different coloured pens, or figures or letters) to show which heading it belongs to, you will then easily be able to make a new list in which the brief notes are grouped together under the appropriate headings (see p. 31). This is the linear approach to initial planning.

Alternatively, you can use the so-called 'sunburst' form of notes, in which you start with main headings, and use 'sunrays' for each of your points within those subjects (see the illustration on p. 30). Some of the 'rays' will develop into 'sunbursts' themselves. The 'sunburst' approach has the advantage of feeling less formal than the linear style, and of not so obviously placing one note in front of another, which sometimes seems to give the first note more importance than it should have, and you may find this helpful when you come to work out the order that you will use. Of course, because you will finally need to have everything in the order that you intend to cover it in the book, you will eventually need to convert your sunbursts into linear lists.

One of the problems which you may find is that some of your material seems to belong under more than one heading – you cannot perhaps entirely divorce your family life

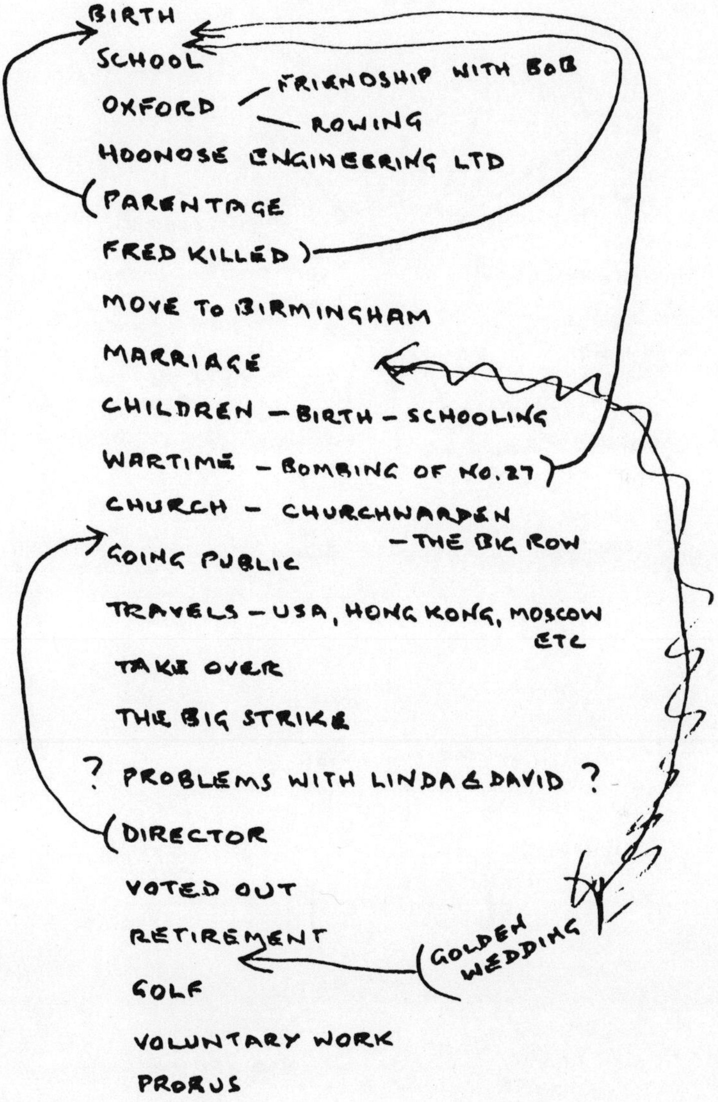

First list of subjects, linear style

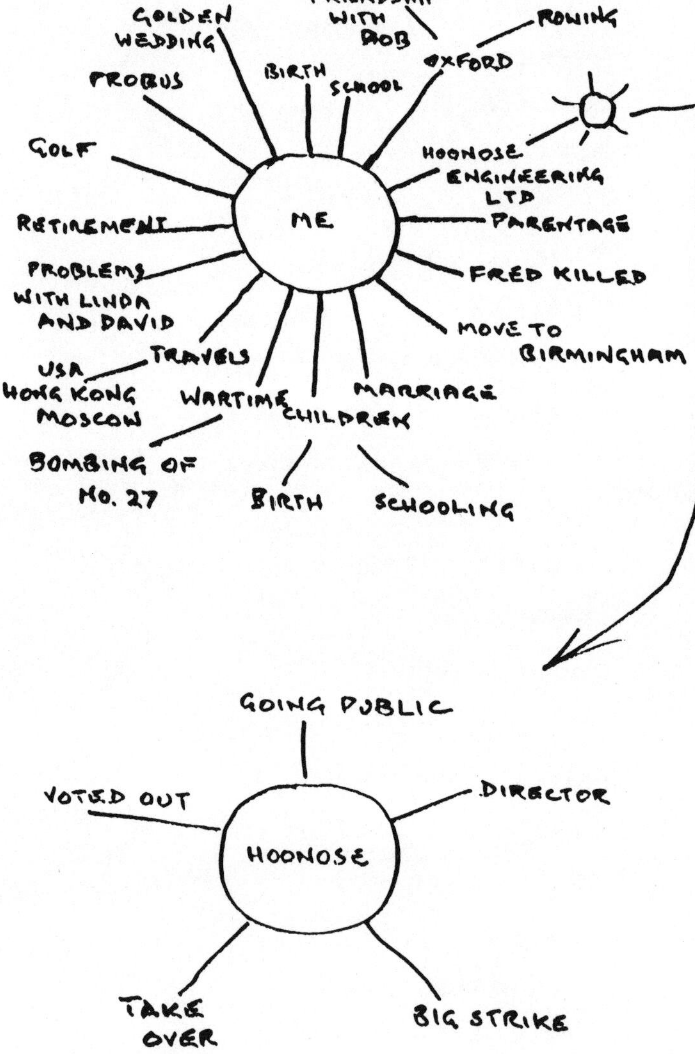

First list of subjects, sunburst style

CHILDHOOD
- BIRTH AND PARENTAGE
- WARTIME – FRED KILLED – NO. 27 BOMBED
- SCHOOL

GROWING UP
- OXFORD – FRIENDSHIP WITH BOB – ROWING
- JOINING HOONOSE
- MEETING MARGARET

HOME LIFE
- MARRIAGE
- BIRTH OF CHILDREN – SCHOOLING – LATER PROBLEMS
- CHURCH – CHURCHWARDEN – THE BIG ROW

HOONOSE
- MADE DIRECTOR
- GOING PUBLIC
- TRAVELS – USA – HONG KONG – EUROPE
- TAKEOVER
- BIG STRIKE
- VOTED OFF BOARD

RETIREMENT
- VOLUNTARY WORK
- CHURCH
- GOLF
- GOLDEN WEDDING

List of subjects amended and re-arranged

from your career, because each had a substantial effect on the other. You may have to rejiggle your headings, or use different ones. And another problem that you may encounter is the odd brief account of an episode or a short divergence into some subject of minor importance which does not seem to fit under any of your headings. The answer may be to omit the passage concerned, or to spend some time working out how you might introduce whatever it may be under an existing heading (which, with a little ingenuity, is usually possible).

When you have a neat list of subjects grouped under headings, you may be able to see each group as providing the material for a chapter (and perhaps its title), and it may be helpful, when writing out your plan, to keep all the material for one chapter in one paragraph – rather like the heading of a Dickens chapter: *Nicholas seeks to employ himself in a new capacity, and being unsuccessful, accepts an engagement as tutor in a private family*. It is possible – indeed, quite likely – that some groups may be too large and will need splitting into two or more chapters, while others will be so slight as to need incorporating with other material.

Length

How long should a chapter be, anyway? There are no rules, but on the whole readers like chapters not to be too long, and once you find yourself producing a chapter of 10,000 words or more, it might be worth looking at the material to see whether it would be better if split to make two or three chapters. At this stage in your writing, when you are simply looking at a list of subjects and headings, you may have very little idea of how many words it will take to cover what you want to say, so a decision on whether to put any particular material into one, two, or more chapters, can be left for the time being. In any case, although it is worth considering the average reader's view that major breaks in the narrative should come at reasonably frequent intervals, in the end the question is one which you may answer entirely as you like. It is often a matter of instinct, and even if you are not a practised writer, you are quite likely to find that you *know* when to leave a chapter as it is, however long (or short) it may be, or whether to manipulate the structure in some differing way.

There is no need to concern yourself at this stage about the total length of the book unless you are seriously hoping that it will be accepted by a commercial publisher (see Chapter 10). In any case, it is much better, whatever your aims, to let the book find its own length. If you try to bump it out just to make it a longer read, the padding will almost certainly show, and will probably bore the reader into the bargain; if you underwrite, the material will seem skimpy, and the reader is likely to feel that the book has no meat in it, and may wonder why you have apparently chosen to conceal so much.

Looking at the Whole Plan

Whatever sort of book you decide to write, prepare a plan, or what might be called a synopsis, for yourself, along the lines already suggested, and don't be afraid to change it and keep on changing it until you have something which seems satisfactory. Planning is often something of a messy business, because ideas don't always come at once in neat little parcels. You may need to write out a number of draft plans before you can move on to the next stage.

When you have got an outline with which you feel satisfied, there is one more important thing to do, and that is to consider it as whole. To quite a large extent we have so far been looking at trees; now is the time to see what the wood is like. Is there a flow to it? As we all know, life is not just a series of disconnected episodes – everything develops from and has links with everything else, and you need in your autobiography to give the reader some feeling of this progress, and indeed you might look to see whether you are also conveying a sense of the development that has taken place in your character – the transition from the inexperience, the enthusiasm, the hopes of youth to the maturity, the understanding and perhaps a little of the cynicism of much later years.

Look, too, to see that your outline has a balance to it. Although it does not always follow, the more space you have devoted in your plan to a particular aspect of your story, the longer that section of the finished book is likely to be, and vice versa. Check to see that you have not overemphasized your childhood at the expense of your youth, for instance, or have planned to write at length about a certain episode in your career (perhaps because you are in fact almost obsessive about it) so that it trivializes the rest.

It may help you to highlight in your plan the most important events that you intend to describe. Are they reasonably spread out? Or do they perhaps nearly all come close together in one particular part of your story? Of course, you cannot distort the chronology of your life, but if you see that there is a lack of this kind of balance in your plan, then perhaps you should consider something which does not follow the normal time sequence so slavishly.

Another concept which might be of assistance is that of trying to see whether there is some kind of theme to your life. Is it a rags to riches story? Or have many exciting things happened to you simply because you were by chance in the right place at the right time? Thinking of ideas of that kind, you may find that you have pegs on which to hang the narrative, progressing from one point to another.

Take Your Time

Even if you have readily accepted the advice to plan before you start writing, you are probably still champing at the bit, wanting to get started, forming sentences in your mind – 'I'm writing my life story' sounds so much more positive than 'I'm going to write my life story, and I'm thinking about it.' But, as I said earlier, thinking and planning are part of writing. They mustn't be hurried. Take your time. When an idea occurs to you, make a note of it, but don't rush to write it up in full (unless you really can't bear to leave it alone); let it lie at the back of your mind. It won't be idle there – as most professional writers will tell you, thoughts about what you are writing don't go to sleep when you're not ready to work on them, because the subconscious gets busy, and will dig up all sort of things, including not only forgotten memories, or a telling phrase which you could use, but perhaps the solution to the problem of how to tackle a difficult part of your story. But the subconscious can't be hurried – it too needs time to work. It also takes time to test out your conscious ideas, to make sure that you really want to use them, to see how they will fit into the general scheme of things, and to make any necessary adjustments.

Take your time. If you ask published authors how long they take to write a book, they will often say, 'Eighteen months – a year thinking about it, and six months actually writing it,' or something of that sort. Of course, authors vary: some do hardly any thinking before they plunge in (not advisable unless you are supremely talented or very experienced), others take years of preparation; some write slowly, while others churn out their books at speed, producing several in a year. If the latter group have thought about their books in advance and used all their writing experience, they will probably maintain a good standard, while with other speedy writers it is often possible to see sloppiness in their work – as Sheridan said, 'Easy writing's curst hard reading'. You will find as you progress through this book that I keep on telling you not to rush things. Writing, especially if you are inexperienced, is a slow, careful process, or should be. In the end you have to find your own time schedule, but I can promise you this: the more time you take to think about and plan your book, the easier it will be to write, when you get to that stage.

3 Research

Your first thought about research may be that you don't need it. Your life story is all in your mind, and even if some of it has become buried over the years so as to be almost inaccessible, once you start to think back, you will remember everything that you need. After all, the book isn't going to record every tiny little detail about you.

This may be basically true, especially the part about being able to dredge up almost forgotten incidents from the past when you give yourself a chance to do so, reminiscing to yourself in a gentle, relaxed sort of way. All sorts of distant recollections will float back into your mind – names of people you haven't seen for years will suddenly leap out of the past, together with an image of the person's appearance and often a scene in your mind's eye of you and the other person on an occasion when you did something or went somewhere together, and it seemed memorable at the time, and now has proved so because you can recall it. However, the older you are, the more likely you are to agree that you won't be able to rely entirely on your memory for everything that you want to write about.

It is always said of the forgetful elderly that they can remember the distant past more easily than something which happened only a short while ago, and there is certainly a lot of truth in that. But with advancing age, the memory, even for those important events and happenings of our youth and young adulthood, becomes a little frail. Just when did that quarrel with your cousin take place, and prove so bitter that you never met again? What was the name of that chap in the warehouse who was so good at mending shoes? If you go farther back into childhood, the things that you remember may be very distinct, but are likely to be distorted because you were small and saw things through childish eyes and did not understand much that went on. So does Yelverton Rock, on the edge of Dartmoor, really tower hundreds of feet into the sky, as you remember it from when you first went there? And how old were you, anyway – three? – or was it four? And were the summers really sunnier then? And why did you suddenly have to come home in the middle of the holiday? A thousand little things like that are almost certain to bother you when you start trying to work out everything about your experiences that you want to say. Some of them will pop back up out of the subconscious without much trouble, but others will elude you. (And if any men are reading this book – sorry, chaps, but we have to admit that we're much worse than the women at remembering details from the past, as that song between Maurice Chevalier and Hermione Gingold in the film musical *Gigi* so cleverly demonstrated.)

Even the fellows can remember a lot of apparently forgotten details if they use triggers. Start thinking about the garden of your childhood home, for instance – for me that conjures up the clump of golden rod near where my father used to stand while letting off fireworks while I watched from indoors, and the runner beans which grew behind the two apple trees at the far end, and I see myself playing tennis by hitting the ball against the back wall of the house, and breaking a window on the landing. Other triggers which can work brilliantly are food, sweets, music, pictures, houses, the furniture of your home, life before central heating (coal fires, oil stoves and chilblains), clothes, public transport, shops, holidays, and the shattering of illusions – discovering that the Father Christmas who filled your stocking was your father – learning about death, realizing that life isn't fair. There are later triggers too – puberty, your first love, school, university, service in the Forces, books, sport, politics, religion, and a host of others.

But you may still need to do some research. It is easy to know where to start – by looking in your diary. At least, it might be if you have kept a proper diary rather than just an engagement book. But it's more than likely that even if you started that sort of diary once you didn't keep it up, and the entries won't be of much help. But you will almost certainly have other papers that you can turn out, such as letters and receipts, birth, marriage and death certificates, wills, old passports (going back to the time when they were always stamped when you entered a foreign country), old programmes, school reports, certificates for passing exams, documents relating to service in the forces, and so on. Even old bank statements or building society accounts books can sometimes provide an essential piece of information. And so, as a matter of fact, can the diary which is no more than an engagement book.

If you do not have many such papers and documents, it is often possible to get replacements, or to examine material kept in archives. Birth, marriage and death certificates can be obtained, at a comparatively small cost, at the General Register Offices in London, Edinburgh and Belfast. Such certificates were first issued in 1837, and became compulsory in 1875, so are available, in most cases, for two or three generations back. Parish Registers can also be consulted – talk to the incumbent of the parish you are interested in. Wills are lodged in the Principle Registry of the Family Division at Somerset House, London. And if you are particularly concerned to find out more about your antecedents in the nineteenth century, the Census returns which were made every ten years from 1841 to 1891 are extremely useful, since they give details of all residents in a given house, including their occupations, ages, and places of birth. The returns are kept in the Public Record Office in London, and can be examined there.

Most schools and universities keep details of past students, and the Navy, Army and Air Force lists are kept at the Public Record Office. All British counties have Record Offices where the local archives may be consulted, and of course every Public Library has a Reference Department from which all sorts of useful information can be obtained, and librarians, whose main function is the retrieval of knowledge, are always delighted to help anyone to find out anything they want to know. There may also be many books in the lending section of the library, such as histories, social histories and biographies, which will be worth consulting. Libraries which specialize in certain subjects or interests are also available for research, and these include collections concerned with various trades and industries. Museums, especially those which are devoted to a particular area or industry, can provide much background material, and in various parts of the country there are what might be called 'Social History Museums', in which various rooms are furnished as they would have been at different periods in the comparatively recent past (and fascinating they are, giving rise to expressions of nostalgia from their visitors – 'Oh, we had a wireless set just like that!' or 'Oh, look! A mangle!'). Newspapers can sometimes be very helpful, and copies of all those printed are filed at the British Library Newspaper Library at Colindale, London. House magazines, parish magazines, society and association newsletters and similar periodicals may be worth consulting, and even in the smallest organizations someone connected with their publication will probably have file copies of their back numbers.

Comprehensive details of all the major research sources can be found in the immensely helpful *Research for Writers* by Ann Hoffmann (published by A. & C. Black), which is the standard work on the subject. The book contains a vast amount of information and also points the way to the more specialized sources which it cannot cover fully.

Whenever possible go in person to any office which may have information that you require, because you are likely to find there a knowledgeable archivist or custodian who will be able to guide you to the right place and who will probably be interested in your research and may from personal expertise be able to supplement the information available in the office. However, it is important to check the opening hours and under what circumstances members of the public may consult the records. You should also be aware that in some cases a charge is made.

But helpful though public records and museums can be, the best place for research will probably be within your family. Don't be afraid to ask your relatives to pass on any memories which will help you. Experts in any subject are nearly always delighted to talk or write about their particular speciality, and of course your family are experts in the subject of themselves. If you have to rely on letters passing between you, you may find that some of your relations are poor correspondents, so go to see them if you can, because almost anyone, given the chance, will be happy to reminisce orally. Indeed, you may have a problem stopping them, especially if the incidents they are telling you about are mainly concerned with themselves; it is not that they are vain, but simply that we all enjoy talking about the past, remembering happy times, raking over old scandals, explaining backgrounds, revealing secrets, and of course contrasting life then with the way it is now. Ask too to be allowed a sight of any family letters which may contain relevant information (but be aware of the copyright situation if you want to quote from any of them – see Chapter 8).

Family reminiscences are fine, but you are quite likely also to need to research into your schooldays or your career, or activities which you have shared with friends, and the advice about seeking information from your relatives applies equally to schoolfellows and teachers, business colleagues and friends.

Photographs too can be invaluable in jogging the memory, often allowing sharper recall of places and friends and relations, and providing you with an instant view of how things looked, how people behaved whenever the photograph was taken – maybe forty or fifty years ago. Indeed, a glance at a photograph of a former business colleague or acquaintance, of whom one has not thought for years, can bring a name instantly to mind. Look at photographs of yourself especially carefully; of course you have seen them dozens of times before, but the more you look, the more the memories will come back, and perhaps the more you will be able to see yourself dispassionately – was that slim figure really me, and does the body language of the way I am standing and looking at the camera reveal that even then I was diffident and shy, or perhaps outgoing and self-confident?

It is often worth looking at your friends' old photographs, if they will turn them out for you. Even though you may not feature in them, a certain scene or the clothes that people in the photos are wearing may jog your memory.

For whatever kind of research you feel a need, do it thoroughly and carefully. It is extremely annoying to find, part way through the actual writing of the book, that you are going to have to go back to one or more of your sources because you forgot some aspect of the subject when you were researching earlier which you now need, or because your note of the matter has turned out to be inadequate. While you are thinking about the book in the early stages, make yourself a list of all the items that you need to check, so that nothing gets forgotten. When using any source for research, write for yourself careful and detailed (and legible) notes of any facts that you are going to use, making sure that they will be entirely comprehensible when you look at them at some later date.

When is the best time to do your research? I believe that as much preparatory work as possible should be completed before you start the actual writing. In that preparation I include not only the planning discussed in Chapter 2, but also research and some consideration of the style in which the book will be written (see Chapter 4). Once you start telling the story, you want to avoid hold-ups as far as you can. It may seem tiresome to spend weeks and even months in what may appear to be non-productive work, but it will make the actual writing very much easier, and will allow you to develop a flow. Having to stop writing in order to ferret out some piece of research is even more tiresome than delaying the writing while you do it in advance.

However meticulously you do your preparatory research, it is quite likely that, in the course of writing, you will come across all manner of things which you have not researched, because you hadn't even thought of them at that stage, and which you need to check. Stop, if you must, but preferably only if the missing information is nagging at you to such an extent that you are suffering from a form of writer's block, and even in that case I would suggest strongly that the best thing to do is simply to skip over that part of the narrative, making yourself a clear note to remind you to research the topic and go back to it when you have finished the first draft of the book. In the end you must please yourself, for there are no rules about writing, but if I were to express a near-rule I would say that you should not let anything interfere with the continuous regularity of the actual writing.

One final comment on the subject of research, which will not surprise you if you have read the previous chapter, is that you should take your time over it. No aspect of writing should be rushed, and digging into your memory, and checking the facts of what you find there, are no exception. Give your subconscious time to work, too, and not only while you are engaged in active research – even when you have gathered together all the information that you think you need, take an extra week or two to mull it over, and your subconscious will probably come up with all sorts of new recollections.

4 Style

Before you begin writing the autobiography you have a number of other decisions to make concerning the style and content of the book.

Do you intend to write factually, telling the complete story of your life and your background (or that part of it which you intend to concentrate on) plainly, without making any attempt to embroider the tale, or are you thinking of producing something which, whether selective or not in content, will be told with a dramatic approach, perhaps including dialogue, and at times using techniques similar to those employed when writing a novel? The answers may depend partly on whether you are going to stick strictly to a chronological account, beginning with your birth, or whether you are going to be much more selective, starting possibly at some moment of change or crisis which will immediately lend drama to the narrative. Both approaches are, naturally, subjective, since you are telling your own story, but the more formal account might be considered as more detached and therefore more objective.

The Autobiography as a Novel

Before progressing to examine the contrast between the two approaches, we should perhaps consider briefly the idea of turning your autobiography into a novel, changing the names of the characters and the locations, and aiming to make it a page-turning story, based firmly on your own experiences. Generally speaking, this is not to be recommended. Autobiographical novels rarely work, and for a number of reasons: they usually stick far too closely to the truth, and since life is untidy, the result is undisciplined – fiction needs to be manipulated into shape; they do not usually read like fiction, but simply as autobiography in disguise; they are often so closely focused on the central character (yourself) that the effect is of something out of balance; the people who read the book and know you and your circumstances may well be embarrassed, especially by any fictional bits that you have added; you may also, however well you have tried to make the characters unrecognizable, be letting yourself in for a libel case. Although, when writing a straight autobiography, some embroidery of the truth may enhance the narrative, as we shall see later, the best advice would be to abandon any idea of fictionalizing the whole story.

The Literary or Poetic Approach

One other different approach should be considered. You might call it the Literary, or even the Poetic, Autobiography. This is the kind of work, already mentioned in Chapter 1, in which the language which is used to evoke the atmosphere of the times and places and circumstances which you are writing about becomes almost more important than the incidents described (although they must, of course, contain more than a modicum of interest). The author needs to have an outstanding gift for language; this will include the ability to pick out *le mot juste*, and to make it and its fellows convey subtle shades of meaning and often a sub-text (by which I mean that the word or words will say more than just their surface meaning); there will also be an awareness of the shape and the inner rhythms of the phrases and sentences. For this kind of writing to work you need, too, a sharp, observant eye, and one which can focus on the essence of the scene or the memory which you want to paint for the reader. If you fancy yourself as another Laurie Lee, have a go. But it's much more difficult than it looks to produce even a pale imitation of the best of this kind of writing, and it doesn't work well unless it is of very high quality. Additionally, it is worth saying that you should not write in this style unless it comes naturally – forced poetic writing is always a disaster.

Will You Use a Formal or Informal Approach?

Reverting to the question of formality and informality, an example of the formal method might begin something like this:

> I was born on the 21st July, 1928, at number 78 Bournevale Road, Ealing, London SW16, at 10.15 a.m. I was the firstborn, and indeed the only child of John Charles Smith and his wife, Mary. My father, himself the third son of Dr William Smith of Nottingham, was working at that time in the Piccadilly branch of the Mercia Bank, where he had met my mother some three years earlier. My mother was the daughter of Henry Archibald Brown, a draper from Broadstairs.
>
> My paternal grandfather had met my grandmother, then Hilda Robinson, when he was acting as a locum at a practice in Derby. Hilda was one of three daughters, all of whom married one of her father's locums. William and Hilda had five children, William, Alice, John, James (killed in the 1914–18 war) and Thomas. My maternal grandfather had married Sarah Wilson, the daughter of a

Broadstairs jeweller. They had seven children, George, Florence, Emily (who died at the age of 6), Arthur, Edwin (who died at birth), Mary and Walter.

Or perhaps the story would start later in life:

It was in the autumn of 1953 that the most significant period in my career began. I had seen an advertisement for the position of senior clerk in Spearum, Ltd, a small company engaged in the manufacture of pig-sticking equipment. Along with several others, I attended an interview, and was pleased when the post was offered to me. Within a year, the firm's Chief Accountant left, and I was promoted to take his place. Thus began thirty-seven happy, productive and successful years.

Alternatively, the first example of an opening given above might be presented in a very different style:

As he put out the stub, the young man waiting in the downstairs room thought to himself, 'I'd better take out shares in Players – they're making a fortune out of me!' It was the fifteenth cigarette he had smoked since the midwife arrived. Why should he be thinking stupid things like that? What was happening upstairs was the important thing! It had been going on for hours. Surely a normal birth should not take as long as this? Every now and then he would hear Mary screaming, and each time he listened to see whether there was a different tone – were the cries getting weaker? Oh, please God, no! He got up and began to pace up and down the room.

Then, suddenly . . . was that a baby's cry? He hurried to the door, to see Doctor Forgan coming downstairs.

'Congratulations,' the old man said. 'You're the father of a bouncing boy. Mother and child both doing well.'

'Oh, thank God, thank God! And thank you, too, Doctor!'

> That young man was my father, John Charles Smith, and I had just made my first appearance in the world.

Or, if you are going to begin at a turning point in your life, it could be written in this fashion:

> 'Any questions?'
>
> We had already covered everything. I thought desperately for a moment, hoping to light upon something which would make me sound bright, eager, responsible. All I could come up with was: 'What are the working hours, sir?'
>
> Mr Spearum looked at me as though I were something the cat (and not a very nice cat) had brought in. 'We don't bother much about keeping strict hours. We work until the job's done.'
>
> I had obviously completely blown my prospects of getting the job.
>
> Nevertheless, and to my astonishment, two days later a letter arrived offering me the position of Senior Clerk at Spearum, Ltd, and thus I began a career which brought me to . . . but, no, I must not anticipate.

Neither of these two approaches is necessarily better than the other, although the later ones both have a slight but welcome touch of humour, and they both use dialogue, which nearly always enlivens a narrative, especially if you can capture something of the characters in it. Which of the approaches appeals to you is a matter of temperament. and depends on whether you prefer the sober or the dramatic. On the other hand, since for the sake of illustration I have exaggerated both the dullness of the first approach and the flamboyance of the second, you may well feel that you don't at all like either of them, and would prefer something either a little less formal than the first examples, or which does not sound like the opening to a romance-filled family saga. Yet another possibility is to use both techniques, so that, for instance, the account of your birth might begin with your father smoking like a chimney and pacing up and down, as in the example above, but would continue:

> . . . I had just made my first appearance in the world.
>
> I was the firstborn, and indeed only child of John Charles Smith and his wife, Mary. My father, himself the third son of Dr William Smith of Nottingham, was working at that time in the Piccadilly branch of the Mercia Bank, where he had met my mother some three years earlier. My mother was . . .

Writing a Humorous Autobiography

If you pride yourself on your sense of humour and know that in conversation you can make your family and friends laugh, you may wish to use an entirely different approach from those we have already discussed, and decide to write a funny book. This is quite likely to cover a period of your life only, because you will be thinking of books like Richard Gordon's *Doctor in the House* and will probably have a whole series of comic anecdotes in mind which will make a book-length account out of a number of comparatively short experiences. There is no reason, of course, why you should not, on the other hand, tell your entire story, from birth to one-foot-in-the grave, in humorous vein.

The one problem in writing a jocular account is whether you can be funny in a way which will appeal to the sense of humour of a wide range of people, and the trap that would-be comic writers most often fall into is of trying much too hard to be amusing. The humorous books which succeed do so by underplaying their comic elements, and one is never aware of the author trying to make the reader laugh. The style of the writing is, of course, important, and to make the most of your jokes and anecdotes you must work on an economy in the telling, and on finding effective punchlines – elements which any professional comedian always uses. But humorous autobiography has a great deal in common with fiction, in that it works best when it is firmly based, not on one-liners, but on the comedy which develops out of character and situation. The writing must be sharp and witty, but the various episodes are funny because of what happens, rather than because of the way the story is told.

One important tip which may help you is that you should never ever precede a comic story with words such as 'What happened next was hilarious.' As soon as an author tells us that an hilarious story is to follow, we tend to react with hopeful anticipation or with scepticism, and the anecdote inevitably fails to work, either because we don't find it as hilarious as the author promised or because we have decided before reading it that we're damned if we're going to be amused. (In a somewhat similar vein, try to avoid using exclamation marks – except in dialogue, when they may be legitimate – because they are usually an intrusion by the author who is saying to the reader, 'Isn't that funny?' or 'Isn't that strange?', and readers much prefer to make up their own minds about such matters.)

The odd touch of humour, rather than any attempt to amuse throughout, may be a better bet. It will add variety, and make you and your book more approachable, it will help to stop you from sounding pompous (if you have a tendency in that direction), and it can often be used to prevent sentiment from deteriorating into sentimentality or awkwardness into embarrassment.

Using the Novelist's Techniques

If you do intend to try to write something a little more exciting than a flat account, it may help you to consider a number of the devices and methods which novelists frequently use, although without turning the work into total fiction, as discussed earlier. This will mean telling the reader about some events in your life with the addition of a little imagination. Imagination is invaluable for the writer of fiction, and there is certainly no reason why you should not use it, or any other of the tools of the novelist's trade.

While it may be legitimate to use your imagination, at least to some extent, while telling your story, beware of attributing thoughts and actions to others when you don't know whether those thoughts and actions actually took place. Guessing of this sort is likely to lead to the use of phrases like 'he would have done this or that', 'she must have considered the question carefully', 'no doubt he went there' and so on, and the nature of these wordings is an attempt to add certainty to a doubtful account. In fact, the reader is quite likely to question the truth of what follows. If you must use that kind of speculation, it is more honest and effective to say, for instance, 'I think that he would probably have done' or 'I feel sure that she must have considered the question carefully', because you are then yourself introducing an element of doubt and making it clear that you are merely giving your opinion.

Even if you intend to use a more formal, chronological approach, but especially if you intend to be more relaxed than that, the various tips and suggestions which follow should help to make your narrative more appealing.

Cliffhangers

The word 'cliffhanger' derives, of course, from the days of the first movies which were often shown in weekly instalments. At the end of one episode the heroine might be clinging on to a cliff for dear life, with a three hundred foot drop and no hope of rescue in sight, and you had to wait until the next week to see how she got out of this perilous situation. The cliffhanger in writing need not be quite as dramatic as that, but it can be used very effectively at the end of a chapter, leaving the story at a critical point in its development and making the reader turn to the next chapter eagerly in order to find out what happened thereafter. In a different medium, some of the best examples of a cliffhanger can be heard on radio each weekday in *The Archers* – every episode leaves you in the middle of some kind of crisis, and you tune in the next day (if you are an addict) to hear the rest of the story. In a novel the cliffhanger works to the greatest advantage if the situation at the end of the chapter is not immediately resolved at the beginning of the next chapter; the novelist moves to a different part of the story and another set of characters, leaving the reader still wanting to know the outcome of the cliffhanger and having to wait for it until the intervening episode has been dealt with (or itself has reached a cliffhanger point). It may be possible for you to use this device in your autobiography, leaving yourself, for instance, at some crisis point in your career ('I opened the door. The policeman asked if I were Mr Brown, and when I nodded said, "I have a warrant for your arrest, sir." '), and using the next chapter to relate events concerning your family which were taking place at the same period in your life, and only after that going back to the false arrest.

Flashbacks

The second trick which novelists find helpful is the flashback, in which the narrative jumps backwards in time to cover some event which took place earlier, before returning to the period from which the jump was made. It is the equivalent of the way we sometimes say, when telling a story, 'I should have told you that . . .', except that in a written narrative you use the device deliberately to create an effect, rather than because you forgot to give your listener some essential background information. Flashbacks are useful, partly because they add variety to the narrative, and partly because they enable the writer to move the story back in order to introduce material which might have seemed irrelevant, and which would probably have taken up more space than it deserved, if it had been dealt with chronologically earlier in the story. Flashbacks can be used effectively to explain events or attitudes, or perhaps to introduce someone whom you decided not to mention at an earlier juncture. You can also sometimes add suspense to the narrative by withholding certain information until the time is ripe for it to be revealed in a flashback.

One major problem with the flashback is that you frequently find yourself using the pluperfect tense, and scattering 'had' all over the place:

> One day, when I was walking down the High Street, I suddenly bumped into Douglas Jones. I had first met him when we had been in the RAF together. I had heard him whistling a snatch of Beethoven one day, and had joined in. We had discovered that we had much in common, and had become friends, and had had many conversations about music. We had lost touch after we had been posted to different places, and had had very different war experiences.

This clumsiness can easily be avoided. Leave the first one or two 'had's' in, but after that use the simple past, adding a sentence at the end of the flashback to indicate that you have reverted to your original time:

> One day when I was walking down the High Street, I suddenly bumped into Douglas Jones. I had first met him when we were in the RAF together. I heard him whistling a snatch of Beethoven one day, and I joined in. We discovered that we had much in common,

> and became friends, and had many conversations about music. We lost touch after we were posted to different places, and had very different war experiences. Now, when we saw each other again, we took off as though we had been meeting regularly through the years.

If you were to begin your life story by describing your present situation, then going back to your birth and working your way forward chronologically, you could claim that virtually the whole book was told in flashback. There is nothing against that, but the flashback, like most things in life and literature, must not be used too often – an occasional, or even a very long excursion into a previous time may work very well, but to keep switching from the present to the past and back again can be distracting and irritating.

Suspense

One of the elements which keeps us reading a novel is our inability to guess exactly what will happen. We may know that a romantic novel will finish with wedding bells for the heroine, or that an adventure story will end with the defeat of the baddies, but we don't know how we shall arrive at that result, going through various unexpected twists and turns on the way. In writing your life story it may be difficult to surprise your close family, who will know quite a lot about your life, but for readers who don't have that intimate knowledge it is worth trying to keep various elements of the story up your sleeve. What you are trying to do is to create suspense, just as an adult does in saying to a child, 'Guess what I've got in my hand.' And then you open the hand, and, oh, what a surprise! You are using this technique of course when you end chapters with a cliffhanger. The main point is not to anticipate the exciting parts of your story. Never write anything like 'This was the turning point in my life which led me on to become the Managing

Director of Spearum Ltd', or 'Little did I know that four years later I would be married with children of my own', or 'surprising events were to follow' (telling your readers that what is to come is going to be surprising, is rather like saying that something is hilarious – they are inclined to find the surprise unsurprising). If you look back at the example of a formal beginning quoted early in this chapter, you will see that the supposed author wrote, 'Thus began twenty-seven happy, productive and successful years.' Well, he didn't give the whole story away, but he came close to doing so, and it's not advisable. Let the reader wait to find out what happened. You can say 'This was a turning point in my life', or 'Little did I know what would happen', but don't tell us more than that at that particular stage. (As a matter of fact, you would do well to avoid 'Little did I know' – it is a very tired cliché.)

Character Studies

The plots of all good novels are based on the characters of the story, and their actions and reactions. People are always interesting, so you should take the opportunity in your autobiography to include character studies of the persons who appear in it. (For that matter, if certain individuals are interesting enough, there is no reason why you should not tell the reader in some detail about them even if they played barely a peripheral part in your story, let alone a more significant role.) You can do this, if you like, in fairly solid pieces each time that a new person enters your narrative, but it is usually better to spread the details out a little so that the reader learns them gradually. Don't tell us everything about such persons when they first appear, but keep one or two pieces of information aside, and drop them in later. This is not only to add some variety to the way you convey information, but because long chunks of factual material are often difficult to absorb fully.

It is in fact far from easy to paint an effective portrait of a character if you rely solely on a description of the person's physical characteristics. Try, when you are thinking about the people who will feature in your story, to remember a particular moment or action or habit or whatever it may be which represents to you their very essence, and then make sure that you present it so that the reader will understand the point you are making. Additionally, remember that in any case, character is best conveyed through actions rather than through descriptions, so it is more effective if you want to indicate that someone is kind, or pompous, or funny to show them being kind, pompous or funny, rather than just telling the reader that that is one of their characteristics. The novelist Ivy Compton-Burnett said, 'People in real life hardly seem to be definite enough to appear in print.' What she was implying, I think, is that in fiction you have to select and perhaps emphasize the aspects of a character which you want to present, and the technique will work just as well for real-life people in a factual book as for imaginary ones.

Action or Narration

Tutors of Creative Writing often use the terms 'Action' and 'Narration'. The former, in this sense, does not necessarily mean physical action, but refers to the description of an episode in detail, as it happens, before the reader's very eyes, as it were; narration, in contrast, consists simply of a statement summarizing what has happened. So, 'They quarrelled bitterly' is narration, but if you show the reader the quarrel from its beginning through to its end, putting in all the dialogue, that would be action. Action nearly always uses a great deal of dialogue, and it exposes the emotions of the characters. It is more exciting than the flatness of narration, and it also takes up a great deal more space. You should use action, rather than narration, whenever possible, for all the more important episodes in your life, allowing the reader to be there with you, making a scene of it. Keep narration for the duller linking material and backgrounds.

Explanations

I said earlier that flashbacks could be used to explain various matters, and explanations are indeed sometimes required. You may need, for instance, to make it clear to younger readers that the much stronger class divisions which prevailed before World War II were widely accepted as normal at that time – people knew their station in life and mostly kept to it – or you may have to tell anyone without your expertise the meaning of various technical terms which you include in your narrative. In general, however, beware of explaining too much. Readers are usually quite bright, and capable of putting two and two together and making four – or even five. They like to work things out for themselves, so try not to state the obvious, or, at the end of some passage, to add an unnecessary sentence summarizing what has just gone before in case the reader didn't get it.

Extraneous Details

Everything in a book should be there for a purpose; every word should be doing a job; every piece of research should be included only because it adds to the story, and not simply to show off its author's knowledge; all waffle should go, and in dialogue you should cut anything which is no more than chit-chat (all those trivial questions and answers which we go through automatically for the sake of politeness, barely listening to what we say or the responses – 'How are you?', 'Very well, thanks. And you?', 'Nice day, isn't it?', etc. Good writing is always spare. This does not mean that there is no room in your book for interesting pieces of information, stories about other people, comments on what was happening in the world at large, even if these matters do not closely involve the subject of the book; given some tenuous connection with the autobiographer, such material can legitimately be included, but it should be written with economy, so that it is not too long before the reader is taken back to the main subject and more personal issues. And it should in fact arise out of the main narrative, rather than being put in merely haphazardly.

Background material may sometimes cause problems. You may wish to include a lot of material about your family, or about the circumstances in which you were brought up, and it may seem sometimes as though all this setting-of-the-scene, essential though it may be, is holding up the main point of the book, and providing a barrier to the potential reader's enjoyment. It is difficult to solve the problem completely, but you may be able to mitigate it to some extent if you follow the advice given earlier in respect of character studies – try not to give all the information in one solid lump, but keep some facts back to be dropped in later in the book.

The Personal Pronoun

One of the problems that you will encounter in writing an autobiography is the number of times that you will be saying 'I' or 'me' or 'my'. It is inevitable, of course, but while you may feel a need to avoid the personal pronoun whenever you can, don't become paranoiac about it, and please don't be tempted into using such alternatives as 'the present writer', 'yours truly', 'your humble servant', which will sound both stilted and coy. Such phrases make it obvious, into the bargain, that you are searching for alternatives, and they become very obtrusive. As for the so-called royal 'we', that should be reserved for the Queen and Lady Thatcher. 'Myself' may seem like an acceptable alternative in many circumstances, but it still has an awkward feel to it, and should really be used only as an emphasis in the phrase 'I myself'. The repetition of 'I' can often be avoided by rephrasing and joining up the sentences in a paragraph so that one 'I' at the beginning will be all that is necessary. Some autobiographers choose to write in the third person to avoid the difficulty, but this always has a distancing effect, as though the author is not really involved.

What you can do is to stop yourself whenever possible from writing things like 'I remember . . .' or 'If my memory serves me right . . .' (which is another particularly tiresome cliché) or 'I now come to . . .' All these phrases are unnecessary, and if you cut them out you will be reducing the number of personal pronouns. Similarly, use names (first names or surnames, with or without titles, as appropriate) for the people who play a major part in the story, rather than referring to them as 'my partner', 'my uncle', 'my boss' (although it will not always be possible to follow this advice because of the context or the need for variety). If you have a wife, do avoid calling her 'the wife', or worse, 'my old woman', or worse still, 'the trouble and strife' (except, perhaps, just once as a joke).

Another difficulty that you may face with the use of the personal pronoun is whether to write 'my wife/husband/partner and I' or 'my wife/husband/partner and me'. Which is correct? Either may be, according to the context. There is a growing tendency to use the '. . . and I' construction all the time, in the apparent belief that it sounds more educated and genteel. In fact, grammatically speaking, 'I' is in the nominative case, while 'me' can be accusative or dative (and in some circumstances, genitive) and correct usage takes account of those facts. You can easily tell which style to use by trying out the relevant sentence but omitting the 'my wife/husband/partner and' part of it; so, if your sentence is 'My wife and I went to the theatre', that is correct, because, leaving out 'My wife and' you would say 'I went to the theatre', not 'me went to the theatre'; in the same way 'He persuaded my husband and I to go to the theatre' is wrong, because you wouldn't say 'He persuaded I . . .', and 'She gave my partner and I tickets for the theatre' is equally incorrect, for a similar reason.

Formal and Informal Writing Styles

Once inexperienced writers begin to produce work which comes under the heading of 'non-fiction', many of them seem to feel a need to be formal in the use of language. If that is what you really want, of course you are entitled to write your book in that style. There is, however, no need to avoid contractions such as 'don't', 'weren't', 'can't', which may often seem more natural (but remember to get the apostrophe in the right place – apostrophes stand for a missing letter or letters, which in the first two examples was the 'o', and in the third were 'n' and 'o'). Equally, if you want to use a great many long words of Latin derivation because you feel that they lend dignity to your prose, go ahead – but don't overdo it, which will make you sound stilted and pompous. The shorter Anglo-Saxon words usually have a much more relaxed and user-friendly feel to them, but to work to the best advantage they need to be offset now and then by the weightier, multi-syllabic words which came to us through Latin and French, because this will give your prose a welcome variety. Slang is entirely acceptable, too, and so nowadays are those so-called four-letter words, which even your elderly relatives are likely to know and to read without being shocked.

Style, which is simply the way you write, is something which worries many inexperienced writers. 'I don't think my style is good enough,' they say. If what you have written conveys your meaning clearly without over-elaboration, and also has a flow and variety to it, so that if you read it aloud it sounds right, then you have no need to worry. Good style always has simplicity, rhythm, variety and, most important of all, clarity, and you have undoubtedly achieved that.

Finding Your Own Voice

Choose any style you like, as long as you are comfortable with it. The last thing you should do is to adopt an approach which is foreign to your nature. Don't be influenced by what other people have done – don't even take any notice of what I say in this chapter (although I hope you will find my suggestions of some use) – but write in the way which comes naturally to you, and stick to it.

You may be thinking that it is all very well to give that sort of advice, but that it isn't particularly helpful for someone who is not used to writing at any length. It may help you more to learn what the publisher Michael Joseph said to Monica Dickens. He had met her at a dinner party, and, hearing her talk of her experiences as a home help, realized at once that she could write an amusing, entertaining book.

He invited her to come to his office to discuss the possibility, and she told him that she wouldn't know where to begin. 'Imagine,' he said, 'that you have just come into a room full of your friends, and you say to them, "You'll never guess what happened to me." And you tell them. That's what you do when you write your story – you tell it to your friends.' He was suggesting what you might call 'an intimate voice'. In an essay included in a book called *Literary Journalism* (published by Ballantine Books, New York), Mark Kramer, professor of Journalism at Boston University, Massachusetts, makes the same point: 'The powers of the candid, intimate voice are many . . .Formality of language protects pieties, faiths, taboos, appearances, official truths. The intimate voice sidesteps such prohibitions . . .It is the voice in which we disclose how people and institutions *really* are.'

How people and institutions really are is one of the things that you must aim at conveying. But remember that Professor Kramer says 'the voice in which *we* disclose . . .' He is personalizing the instruction – it is through *your* eyes and *your* voice that we must be shown the people, the institutions, the events in your life. To make people understand what it was like to live your life you must not simply tell them what happened, but describe, especially for anything which may be outside the average reader's knowledge, how you felt, both mentally and physically, what you thought, what made the moment memorable. Allow us to share your experience.

Writing with Authority

This chapter contains a number of suggestions which may or may not be useful in writing the book in the style that you prefer. I hope that, even if some of the ideas do not appeal to you, you will consider them very carefully. When you have decided either to accept or refuse the various suggestions, you will then be able to undertake the writing with a certainty of what you are doing, and it is this which will give your work an authority. If you look at the first few lines of any book by a successful author, especially one who has a reputation for quality, you will be aware straight away of a sense that the book is under control, that the author knows what he or she is doing. This is the authority of which I speak, and my object is to enable you to feel it and write with it.

5 Writing Methods

Where to Begin

Usually, when I am writing a book, I like to begin at the beginning and work my way through until I get to the end, but occasionally, especially if I am feeling a little anxious about the opening pages, I will start by writing a chapter about which I feel entirely at ease. I tend, once that chapter is drafted, to go back to the beginning, because if I continue to write only the easier chapters, the spectre of that opening will grow larger and larger, and I shall be more and more reluctant to tackle it. Besides which, the more of a book that I write out of order, as it were, the more likely I am to end up with chunks of text which do not hang together, which are repetitious, which contain material appearing in the wrong place – in short, I shall have produced confusion.

There is nothing to stop you writing your material in any order you like, and it certainly helps to start with something which you know is going to flow readily. But if there is a section which you are not looking forward to writing, don't leave it too long, but have a go at it once you have got yourself at least part way into the mood. Equally, although I would always advise any writer to leave the major revision of the typescript until the first draft is complete (see Chapter 6), there is nothing to stop you from going back to the work you have produced to insert new material.

Writing Materials

You can write with a pencil, a biro or pen, in any colour you want, or on an old-fashioned typewriter, or on a newer one which has a limited word processing facility, or on a computer, using a word-processing programme. You can use notebooks or writing pads or separate sheets of paper. It doesn't in the least matter which of these methods and materials you prefer; the choice is yours, and you should use whatever you are comfortable with, and if you do not have a computer there is no need to go out and buy one just to write an autobiography. Yet another alternative is a tape recorder or similar device into which you dictate your story (although you will need to find someone to type it up for you) – or you could, of course, dictate directly to a secretary, even, if you so wish, lying on a chaise-longue as you do so, in the manner of Dame Barbara Cartland.

You will need at some stage to produce typewritten, rather than handwritten, material, especially if you are going to submit the work to a publisher, but also if you are producing the work simply for your immediate family to read – don't expect them to struggle through a handwritten manuscript. However, it is not essential to own even a typewriter, let alone a state-of-the-art computer, because there are many willing typists around, and if there is no one in your own family with the ability to turn your manuscript into a typescript, dozens of professionals advertise regularly in the pages of magazines for writers, offering to produce from your material both 'hard copy' (jargon for a typescript) and a disc (which many publishers would require if they decided to publish your book – see Chapter 7). The prices which these helpful people charge are not enormous. Moreover, while you should not inflict your handwriting on your nearest and dearest, there is no need to worry whether such a typist would be able to read your scribbled words; many of them have been coping successfully for years with the almost totally illegible scripts with which they have been presented.

If you are intending to produce your own hard copy, or to persuade a relative or friend to do so, you will find instructions about the way it should appear in Chapter 7. A professional typist will know these rules (although it won't do any harm to check that the one you have chosen is used to publishers' requirements).

In Chapter 7 you will read that typescripts should be typed in double spacing on one side of the paper only. I would strongly advise that you should follow those rules even for your early drafts, because they make your work much easier to read and to correct. I think it is also always worth using A4 paper of a reasonable substance and quality.

When and Where to Write

You may have read of writers who tidy their desks, sharpen pencils, re-pot the geraniums, clean their tennis shoes – anything rather than get down to writing. I suspect, however, that this applies most often when the authors are about to begin a new book, because the first pages are nearly always difficult. So don't be discouraged if you find writing a struggle at first, even if the problem persists for quite a time. Persevere. You need to get into the swing of it, and once you do, everything will get easier, and the words will start to flow, and you will end a writing session with reluctance, and look forward to the next one.

One of the lessons that many professional writers have learnt is the importance of writing regularly. Mary Wibberley, author of a large number of highly successful romantic novels, talks of 'the writing muscle in your mind'.

She says that it is like any other muscle – if you don't use it, it becomes stiff and doesn't work properly, but the more often you exercise it, the better it will perform. She is right. Charles Dickens was telling us the same sort of thing when he said, 'If I miss writing for one day it takes me a week to get going again.' So get the habit. Organize your life, so that you have a regular time every day when you can write, even if it is for a very limited period – you will be surprised how much you can get done in a quarter of an hour, if you do it regularly. You may say that you would be only too pleased to organize your time if you had any to spare. There are two answers to that: the first is that if you want to do something badly enough, you can always squeeze it into a busy life somehow; and the second is to get up a quarter of an hour earlier each day, or go to bed a quarter of an hour later – or both – and use that time for writing.

A further advantage of writing at a regular time is that your husband, wife, partner or any other variety of family (assuming that you do not live on your own) will get used to your stints and learn to leave you alone while you work. This is more important than you may think, because most non-writers find it very difficult to think of writing as work (which it is), demanding application and concentration, so you need to train those you live with to respect your writing sessions (and preferably to bring you, silently, cups of tea or coffee while you slave away).

Find the time of day that suits you best. This may need a certain amount of experimenting, although it is possible that you are already well aware of the way your mental clock works. Perhaps you know, or will discover that you are more alert and that the words flow comparatively easily in the afternoon, while earlier in the day you don't always seem to be fully awake, and in the evening you find it difficult to concentrate and tend to drop off. Or it may be that the morning, or late at night, will be right for you. Some authors like to write late at night, or really early in the morning, when everyone else is in bed, but that may have more to do with needing peace and quiet than with whether you are a lark or an owl. Experiment until you discover the part of the day when, as a writer, you are in your best functioning mode.

Because you will not be at your desk for every moment of every day, it is a good idea to have a notebook and pencil always available so that you can at any time write yourself a note about something which has just occurred to you which you want to include or perhaps change in your book. For that matter, you will often need the notebook while you are in fact at your desk, because you may get an idea which is not immediately connected with what you are working on at that moment, but which will need to be remembered for another time. Without a notebook it is all too easy to forget. Do make sure that the note is both legible and that you have written sufficient to be able to recognize what you were thinking of.

Trick or Treat

Because the human mind, despite its enormous complexity and scope, can sometimes be fooled by childish tricks, I would like to suggest that you should make some little rules for yourself. Firstly, always write, if you can, at the same time of day. Secondly, write, as far as possible, in the same place. Some professionals, like the late Catherine Cookson, write in bed, Michael Gilbert writes on the train, Barbara Cartland, as already mentioned, dictates her books while lying on a chaise-longue, Bennett Cerf worked it all out, if you will pardon the phrase, while sitting on the lavatory, and others write in the kitchen, in the bath, in a study or even in an office separate from their homes. It doesn't matter where. But you are more likely to write while you are sitting down, rather than standing or lying, and I want next to suggest that you should keep one chair just for that purpose. And, fourthly, if you write in longhand, have a special pen or pencil which you use only on your book. Paper, too – whether you write in longhand or on a machine, always use the same stack of paper, and don't use it for anything else. Then you start playing your childish trick on your own brain by saying, 'I'm sitting in my writing chair, at my writing time, with my writing pen and my writing paper – what on earth can I do but write?' And then get down to it. It can work a treat.

Another trick which you may find helpful is to count the number of words you write each day. It is something which I always do. If the total that I have achieved on a particular day is a poor one, then I try to do better the next day, and even if I've done well, I will try to better it. This acts somehow as a spur to get down to it. And it does not necessarily mean that because I am trying to produce a great number of words they will be of poorer quality; I am simply making sure that I concentrate a little more carefully and don't allow myself to be distracted. I also set myself a weekly target, and this works in just the same way.

'But supposing,' you may ask, 'I don't feel like writing on a particular day. What then?' The answer is to be found in my favourite quotation about writing, which came from the American humorist and poet, Peter de Vries, who said, 'I write only when I am inspired. And I see to it that I'm inspired at 9 o'clock every morning.' Persevere, and make yourself write whether you are in the mood or not. If the work that you produce in those circumstances is poor, then you can revise it later. The important thing is to keep going. Especially, don't give up when you are half way through your book, and have begun to think to yourself that what you have written is boring and that no one would want to read it. That is something that most professional writers feel at some stage during the writing of a book. You just need to battle on, and you will soon get a second wind. As I have already said, regular writing is vital. An American writer once said, 'The only way of writing is by applying the seat of the pants to the seat of the chair.' And you might do worse than pin up a notice with the legend 'It Won't Write Itself!'.

6 Revision

The Professional and the Amateur

One of the differences between professional and amateur writers is that the former revise their work and the latter don't. You may say that you are not a professional, and don't want to be one anyway, and that you will manage without revision, thank you very much. But only a genius can produce perfect work the first time, and there aren't many geniuses around. If you have the chance of looking at the manuscript of any of the great literary classics, you will find that they have been substantially revised (unless they are by writers like Dickens, who didn't have the time to spend on such niceties). Those lines of deathless poetry, which sound so spontaneous and which obviously floated into the poet's consciousness and were written down without a syllable being altered, turn out to have been worked on over and over. Revision really is worth doing, and however much it may add to your labour, it is important not to skimp it.

When to Revise

I would urge you not to begin revising until the first draft of your book is complete. You can of course make minor amendments as you go along, but to do a proper job of revision it is necessary to be able to see the book as a whole. You may think it would be a good idea to write a page or two and then polish them, or even rewrite them. This may make you feel good, because you can assure yourself that you are producing work of a high standard, but it also makes your progress very slow, and you cannot look at the book as a whole to see how everything fits in and works (or does not do so). What about revising after you have completed the first chapter? The problem with that is not only that again you cannot take an overall view, but that you may decide that it still isn't right, and rewrite it. And rewrite it. And rewrite it. And before you know where you are, you have landed yourself in the Permanent Chapter One Revision Syndrome, and your book will never progress beyond that chapter. No, wait until you've got to the end.

Many writers feel that the most laborious part of writing is producing the first draft. Planning may be hard work, but fun too, as you manipulate your material into a satisfactory shape, and prepare to begin the writing with the knowledge of where you are going and how you are going to get there, but the actual writing – putting the words down on paper – is much more difficult, as you search for the best way to express all the thoughts in your mind. It is also less enjoyable because it is, at least to some extent and for some people, an almost mechanical process – a matter of getting the story down on paper (or on the disc) without bothering a great deal about whether it is effectively told. Like many authors, I try to get it over as soon as possible, ignoring any question of the quality of the prose, or whether I am repeating myself, or telling my readers things they know already, or going to the other extreme and forgetting that they don't know certain facts which I have omitted to explain. Revision is when you become godlike, and mould your text to something more in the nature of what you meant to write in the first place, and it can give you great pleasure as you see yourself improving the interest in the story, making everything tighter and more economical, adding subtler nuances, finding the right word and putting it in the right place, correcting all your little mistakes, and so on. Revision can be a really rewarding exercise in its own right.

First, however, if you can bear to do so, put the book away for a while. You may be itching to get on with it, and feeling just in the mood, but a week or two won't matter. Give yourself a little holiday from the writing. There are two purposes for this delay. The first is to distance yourself from your work as far as possible. When you have just finished the first draft, you are too close to it to make any judgements which will be valid. The time lapse helps you to see your work more objectively. The second purpose is to give your subconscious a little freedom to see whether it can come up with anything interesting while your conscious mind is dormant – and it probably will.

How Often to Revise

It isn't easy to revise a book in one go, because there are too many things which need to be examined. I recommend four revisions. That may sound like an awful lot of extra work, but it isn't all that difficult, and will certainly repay the efforts you make. Nor is it particularly boring, because in each case you will be attacking the work in a different way, looking for different aspects of the writing. To confuse matters slightly, before I begin to explain the four different revisions, I should point out that they don't always work out as neatly as the way I describe them. Some of the things I suggest you should do during the second revision you may already have done in the first, and vice versa (the first two revisions are particularly liable to this kind of overlapping), so you don't have to be too rigid about the whole process.

The next point to bear in mind is that after each of the revisions you may have to do a certain amount of tidying up. You may, for instance, have decided to cut your description of a certain event, but have referred to it elsewhere in the book, and you will need to make a further amendment accordingly. Or you may cut a paragraph because the passage is just too wordy and slow-moving, but will then have to rewrite the beginning of the next paragraph so that it follows on seamlessly from the paragraph before the cut.

Taking Your Time

One other recommendation of great importance is that you should take your time over revision. It is not something to be rushed through – each stage may require several readings of pages or chapters, and may also involve you in a fair amount of rewriting. Think carefully about the book, both as a whole and in detail, as described below, and keep on asking yourself whether what you have written is as good as you can make it, or has the potential to be better. You may need to leave some days between revising one part of the book and the next – regularity is not nearly so important as when you are writing – and then go back over what you have already done to pick up the context clearly. You may also discover that certain chunks demand to be rewritten, and the time to do that is straight away, before you forget what is wrong with the first version. You may even decide that the whole thing is awful and that you should start again from the beginning. But never destroy the original wording, because sometimes, after struggling to produce a better way of expressing whatever it may be, you may come to the conclusion that you cannot really improve on your very first attempt. Be patient, take it slowly, and never begrudge the amount of time that your revision takes.

The Length of the Book

Even before you start on the revision of the first page, there is another question to ask yourself, and that is whether the book is of the right length. Perhaps this may seem of importance only if you are hoping to find a publisher for the book (see Chapter 10), but in fact the length of the text will usually give an important clue to the form of the first revision. Make a calculation of the extent of the book in words, which you can do in three stages: firstly, by counting the number of words in a series of full lines to arrive at an average number of words per line; secondly by multiplying that figure by the number of lines on a full page to arrive at the average number of words per page; and thirdly, by multiplying the words per page figure by the number of pages in the book. If you are working on a computer, your word processing programme almost certainly has the facility to tell you how many words you have written. The figures will differ because the former method (which is the one used by publishers) assumes that there are no short lines and no pages which are less than full, whereas the word processor will count the actual words. However, for our present purposes either figure will do. As a rough guide, if your total is less than 30,000 words, it is probable that you have under-written, and will need to expand your material, whereas if your total is edging up to 100,000 words or more, it is likely that you have over-written and will need to cut. Please note: this is no more than a possible indication of work to be done – it may be that the account you want to give of yourself will not cover all the minutiae of your life, and will be all the more effective for its brevity; alternatively, you may have so much to tell that, even compressing the material and writing as economically as possible, you will have difficulty in keeping the narrative down to a quarter of a million words. There are no firm rules about length, but it is a matter of which you should be aware.

The First Revision

The first revision is one in which you should take a broad view. It is concerned with such matters as structure, the economy or extravagance with which you have written, the need to maintain a good pace in your narrative without passages which allow the book to sag, and the question of whether you have included everything you intended to be in the book, or, in contrast, whether you have been lured into writing about matters which are irrelevant, or which you really want to keep to yourself. This is also the time when, whether you have taken the formal or the informal approach, you ask yourself whether you have used storytelling techniques to the best advantage.

If you have followed the advice in Chapters 2 and 4, and especially if you have planned with great attention to detail, it is possible that you will find comparatively little to do in this first revision, but since the theory (represented by planning) is often very different from the practice (the actual writing), it will be worth spending some time on it.

The First Step

Begin your revision by reading the whole book through, not trying to do so quickly (that comes later), but at a fairly leisurely pace, probably taking several sessions to get to the end. Try as hard as you can to separate yourself from the book, and to read it as though it is someone else's story, taking as analytical a view as possible. This is rather easier to do than you might think, although you already know the content, if you have put the work on one side for two or three weeks. Look out for the kind of points mentioned above, and ask yourself questions like these:

Trying to look at the shape of the story as you have told it, is it balanced, or have you, perhaps, spent too much time on one part of your life to the detriment of the rest?

Does the story flow smoothly, and move from one high point in your life to the next in a logical progression?

Are there dull bits (if you think any part of the narrative is boring, it probably is), and have you avoided the inclusion of extraneous details which are not really relevant?

Is there anything which is confusing (remembering that some of your readers will not have your background knowledge)?

On the other hand, have you included unnecessary explanations, not only of things which your readers are certain to know, but of matters which they would be capable of working out for themselves?

Does the narrative ramble from time to time, so that you begin to write about this or that subject and then wander off on to something else and never complete what you originally intended to say? This could apply to a single sentence, or to a whole chapter.

Have you managed to insert some humour, and does it work, or does it seem laboured?

Have you had any success in surprising the reader (even those who know you and your life intimately can be surprised by little snippets of information which they have not heard before)?

If you have used dialogue does it sound natural and as though it belongs to the people who are speaking?

Are the character studies lacking in the kind of unusual

angle or information which will bring the subjects to life, or so smothered in detail that they have become bogged down?

Have you made the best possible use of any tricks like cliffhangers, flashbacks, action and narration?

Does the book have variety, not only in pace and perhaps the use of different approaches and techniques, but in the content?

Above all, have you succeeded in writing the kind of book which you intended?

This is also the time to think again about the length of the book, to cut if it has sprawled a bit too much, or to expand if it's on the short side. Any new material which you add must be relevant – padding inserted simply to make the book an acceptable length is always obvious, even to inexpert eyes, and the reader will quickly get bored. But, if you dredge a bit in your memory, there are usually incidents which you have not included, or telling details about those which you have, and with material of that sort you can expand without risk. It is far more likely that you will need to cut, because most of us tend to over-write, once we have the bit between our teeth, as it were (indeed you may find the opening chapters, when you were still feeling your way, are skimpy in relation to the later ones, when you have got into the flow). Even if you are not particularly worried about the overall length, it is rarely a mistake to cut quite ruthlessly, provided, of course, that you do not eliminate essential information.

Noting Necessary Changes

As you are reading through your manuscript or typescript or are scrolling down your screen, keep a notebook by your side, and write yourself a reminder of anything which you want to change or simply to look at again to see if it can be improved. This is a much better way of working than to keep stopping to make the alterations, because at this stage you are trying to look at the whole book, and that is difficult if you stop and start. But do make sure that your scribbled notes are legible and include the page number to which they refer, and give sufficient detail to bring to mind exactly what it was that made you decide that something needed attention.

The Next Stage

At the beginning of this chapter I suggested that it was not a good idea to revise a chapter at a time, but to wait until you could look at the book as a whole. In this first revision you should certainly begin by going through the whole book, but when you have read it through, made your notes, and carried out any necessary alterations, it is then time to take another look at the text (still as part of the first revision) chapter by chapter, asking the same questions, and making any further changes that seem necessary. The narrative may require a little tidying up afterwards, and you could then, if you want to, read the whole thing through again (and give yourself a pat on the back for having improved it so much).

The Second Revision

You are now ready to tackle the second revision. In the first revision you were looking at the wood – now you are going to look at the trees, and there is a whole forest of them to be considered. Every word, every sentence, every paragraph needs to be examined carefully to see whether it is doing an effective job, and there are many faults which you might look for.

Adjectives and Adverbs

One of the first things I always look at in my own writing is the adjectives and adverbs. Are there too many of them? The answer for me, and for most other writers, is invariably 'yes'. We try to enliven our material by adding far too many adjectives and adverbs, and often, instead of enriching the writing, they make it seem over-lush. Cut them out wherever you can. The best writing is always lean and spare, and the adjectives or adverbs which may appear in it are usually very few in number and have been most carefully chosen. As an exercise, if you feel like trying it, write a description of a short journey – from your home to work, perhaps, or to go shopping – without using a single adjective or adverb. It is quite difficult, but the result can be a strong, sinewy piece of prose. And then try putting in just one adjective or adverb, choosing it carefully and placing it as effectively as possible, and you will see what strength it gains by being on its own.

Repetitions

Look out for repetitions. A word which is repeated just after you have used it is inclined to jar, and since we have a language with enormous resources it is generally possible to replace it with an alternative. But don't be obsessive about this so as to make the reader conscious that you are constantly seeking to find new ways of saying the same thing. Although you want to avoid repetitions, you can't always do so. And sometimes repetition can be an effective device, when you use it deliberately – 'I laughed when I first read the letter and came to the bit about payment, I laughed when he phoned and said he had meant every word of it, I laughed when I met him and discovered that he really was in earnest' – those repetitions of 'I laughed when I' are creating a special effect. Something else that you can repeat without fear is the simplest of the attributions in dialogue – 'he said', 'she replied', 'I asked' – readers will not notice such repetitions, so there is no need to search for alternatives, especially such clumsy examples as 'he gritted', 'she exploded', 'I questioned', which become very obtrusive.

Repetition can also occur, sometimes at considerable length, when you relate an incident or cover some subject of particular interest to you, and then later in the book, quite forgetting that you have already described it, you repeat it, often word for word. It is the equivalent of the stories with which we bore our friends, carrying on relentlessly even when we have begun by saying, 'Stop me if I've told you this before', and ignoring their murmurs to the effect that we have indeed done so, and many times. Such duplications of effort in your book must, naturally, go.

Another repetition which writers of autobiographies are particularly prone to is in the use of 'then' or 'And then'. 'Then I did this', 'Then I did that', 'And then I went to . . .', and so on. Do your best to eliminate them and find another way of moving from one experience to the next. Often it is easiest just to cut 'And then', since the flow of the narrative will tell the reader that whatever it may be is the next thing that happened. 'Then' in those examples is usually simply a habit word – a word which you use regularly without really thinking about it. Habit words are always a pain, losing their value by constant over-use. At least most of us avoid using 'you know' when we're writing. But I have to be on my guard about 'clearly' and 'obviously', with which I am inclined to pepper anything I write. Watch out for your own habit words.

Repetitions are also to be found in the rhythm of your sentences, and you should make sure that you have not dropped into a style in which all the sentences are of roughly the same length and construction. This is often most readily noticed if you read your work aloud – you can hear yourself repeating the same rhythm over and over again. The solution is often simply to connect two such sentences with 'and' or 'but', although sometimes it may be necessary to do a bit of rewriting.

Fine Writing

You can, of course, write in any style you like, but, as I suggested in Chapter 4, you need to be sure of your ability if you are going to attempt a literary or poetic autobiography. If you are not writing that sort of book, you may have been tempted every now and then into 'fine writing', and that is usually a mistake, simply because it is an attempt by the author to show off. Similarly, you may have tried to impress by the use of long words, and especially those of romance language origin. Good style is usually simple, and, as has already been said in an earlier chapter, although one needs some long words of Latin derivation to add variety to the prose, the short Anglo-Saxon vocabulary is usually preferable.

Ambiguities

Clarity is one of the attributes of the very best writing, and you should do everything possible to ensure that your meaning is always clear. Ambiguities are always to be avoided, and many are the result of woolly thinking on the author's part, or because while the thought is clear, the words chosen to express it are not. Sometimes they are the result of the use of a pronoun such as 'he' when two males have been referred to immediately before, and it is uncertain to which of them this 'he' refers. At other times the problem is of not having chosen words which convey a sufficiently precise meaning. And then there are the words and phrases which plague those of us who are, like Dennis Norden, literalists – 'Dogs must be carried on the escalator', for instance, so what do you do if you haven't got a dog to carry? And what has frightened all those entrances which proclaim 'These doors are alarmed'? We all know what is meant, but while it may be fun to mock public notices, you don't really want people distracted from your book by ambiguities of that nature.

Name-dropping

Beware of name-dropping. You may have met a lot of famous people during your life, but should not have put them into your life story unless they have a part to play or you have a good story to tell about them and the occasion when you met. Otherwise they will make you sound boastful and snobbish. Cut them out.

Inconsistencies and Forgetfulness

Since our memories tend to become slightly unreliable and erratic as we get older, you may find that you have provided the reader with two different descriptions of the same episode, or two different dates, or names or whatever it may be, and these must be tidied up.

Malapropisms

Even the most practised of writers can sometimes get confused about the meaning of comparatively rare words, and while you may not go as far in absurdity as Mrs Malaprop, it is comparatively easy to make this kind of mistake. If you are not absolutely sure about a word you are using, the solution is to look it up in a dictionary.

Clichés

It really is a shame about clichés. When they were first coined they were bright and shiny and they expressed something in the most vivid terms. What could be more accurately descriptive than 'as busy as a bee' or 'as cool as a cucumber'? And we all know what we mean by 'giving free rein to something' or 'looking a gift horse in the mouth'. Nearly all our favourite clichés are similes or metaphors. It is extremely difficult to eliminate them altogether, especially since they act as a very useful kind of shorthand – a cliché with a good clear meaning may save us a paragraph of explanation. Nevertheless, if you can avoid using them, do so, because their frequent presence will make your writing seem much more tired than it really is.

Punctuation, Grammar and Spelling

Punctuation, spelling and grammar are the tools of the writer's trade, or some of them, and like any good craftsman or craftswoman a writer should take care of such tools. Some people have never had the benefit of being taught such subjects, and others have resisted, whether deliberately or not, learning them. Ten years ago now the publisher of this book asked me to write one called *The Nuts and Bolts of Writing*, to be primarily about punctuation, grammar and spelling, simply because he was so fed up with the large numbers of illiterate typescripts which flowed into his office. I wrote the book, and it has been in print ever since and has sold well. I am not sure whether it resulted in any improvement in the standard of books submitted, but it is, although I say it myself, a very useful book for those who have difficulties in this direction. If you find punctuation, spelling and grammar difficult, but don't want to bother with my book, or find it less helpful than I say it is, then the answer for you will be to get a friend to help you. It really is worth doing – grammatical and orthographical mistakes can be very off-putting to literate readers, while poor punctuation can often distort the meaning of what you have written.

I cannot leave this subject without mentioning the mistake which, when reading unpublished work as a tutor or as a publisher's reader, is the one I most frequently encounter, and which most irritates me. This is the inability to distinguish between 'it's' and 'its'. The former is short for 'it is' or sometimes 'it has', while the latter is the possessive form of 'it'. So 'it's mine' or 'it's been raining', are correct, but 'this book has lost it's jacket' is not, and should be 'this book has lost its jacket'.

Breaking up Long Passages

I have already suggested earlier in this book that readers are not over-fond of very long chapters, and the same applies to paragraphs. If you see that some of your paragraphs extend over much more than a page of typescript, see if you can break the material into shorter chunks. A paragraph is a collection of sentences all of which are on the same theme, rather like a Christmas parcel in which the presents are all related, as it were, since they are for various members of the same family. If a parcel is to big for the post, you would probably split it into two parcels, perhaps putting presents for the parents in one, and those for the children in the other. My simile has become a bit strained, but you will, I hope, see what I mean.

The Third Revision

Now that you have looked at the wood in the first revision and the trees in the second, and have done whatever tidying up is necessary, you are ready to move on to revision number three, and you will be pleased to know that this is going to be much less of a chore than the first two. It consists of reading the whole book aloud, and in some ways it is the most important of all the revisions, because the ear is so much better an editor than the eye. The best thing, if you can persuade anyone to do it, is to get someone else to do the reading, while you listen. This has great advantages because a stranger will simply read what is on the page, not knowing what thoughts lay behind it when you wrote it. So sometimes you will hear something which has come out with the wrong emphasis, or without the stress on a particular word which makes sense of the whole sentence. Your reader may also stumble over clumsily written prose, and it's very helpful to become aware of matters of that sort. I have already mentioned the question of repetitive rhythms in the sentences, and this is when they will become apparent. Equally, when your writing has been working well, you will be able to hear its flow, and the authority with which it has been written, and that is a very gratifying sensation.

If you cannot badger anyone into reading for you, then read the work aloud yourself – you will still hear things that you missed when you read only with your eyes, and you will also probably pick up some typing errors which have previously remained invisible. When you are reading, and especially if someone else is reading for you, it is important not to stop, at least until you come to the end of a chapter, because you lose the sense of an ongoing narrative, and the rhythm of the prose within the paragraphs and sentences. Again, it is a matter of having paper and pen or pencil at hand, and making quick notes of anything that needs attention, not forgetting to record the page. This does not mean that you should read the whole book at a sitting – again, take your time, so that you listen carefully and thoughtfully.

The Fourth Revision

The first three revisions have all taken a considerable length of time (or should have done so if you want them to be really effective). The fourth revision, in contrast, is a very quick one, taking only a few hours. It is when you read the whole book to yourself in one sitting. Its value is that, at least for most people, it is the only occasion when you manage to hold the entire work in your mind at the same time. It is surprising how repetitious material for instance, can have slipped through despite the earlier revisions, or that something which you intended to be in the book turns out not to be there, and because you have been concerned with the way that you wrote the book, its shape and its style, you may not even have noticed that you forgot to include that particular item. It is a good idea to re-read your synopsis before you start in order to remind yourself of your original intentions.

To carry out this revision effectively, you really need solitude. If you are fortunate enough to have a partner, you need to bribe or cajole that person into guarding you so that you don't have to answer the door or the telephone, and it is even better if whoever it is can be persuaded to provide you silently with food and drink while you are in the midst of the book. If you have no one who can help you in that way, it may be possible to go to the reading room of a public library, or to some other place where you will not be bothered.

Finally

When you have carried out any changes dictated by your four revisions, and done the necessary tidying up, please don't revise again. You may not be satisfied with your book, and may be tempted to go through it yet again. Don't. Four revisions should be enough for anyone, and if you go on you will be slipping into a worse version of Permanent Revision of Chapter One Syndrome – the simpler sounding but more virulent disease, Permanent Revision Syndrome. Your book is now ready to go to the press, or to be submitted to a publisher.

However, if you are really not quite happy with the typescript as it stands, and especially if you feel that it is slow-moving and lacking in excitement, there is just one more revision that you could do, and that is to go through trying to take out an additional 5 per cent of the text. That is not very much, amounting on average to one-and-a-half lines per A4 page. If you don't make the target, well, never mind – if you have managed to cut a word or two here, a paragraph there, perhaps even a whole page once in a while, then you will be surprised by the extra sparkle you have imparted to the narrative. But that really is all that you should do, and that really is the last revision. NO MORE!

7 Preparing the Final Copy

The Typescript

When you have finished writing and revising, you will need to prepare a clean copy for submission to a publisher, or to a printer if you intend to self-publish, or for photocopying if you want only a few copies for circulation among your relatives and friends.

There are few rules about writing, but most of those that do exist are concerned with the way a typescript should be prepared. Always use double spacing – not even 1½ – *double* spacing, on one side of the sheet only, using A4 paper. The paper should be of a reasonable quality – not necessarily the thickest, but certainly not flimsy. Make sure that the typing or printing is black and legible, rather than appearing in a faint shade of grey (so don't use the draft mode on the printer attached to a word processor, except for your personal use). Leave good margins of at least one inch or two and a half centimetres all round, and try to keep the same size margins on every page. If you have the facility on your word processor, it doesn't much matter whether you justify the type or not (although I think most publishers still prefer justification on the left side only).

If you are using a word processor, use a straightforward font, such as Times, or Bookman Old Style or Garamond, and in a reasonably large size, rather than anything pretty but less legible. Don't type the whole work in italics, but use them only when necessary for such things as the titles of books, or for emphasis. Equally, if you are using a ribbon, stick to black – don't use any fancy colours. Try always to keep to the same number of lines on a page (except the first page of a chapter, which will probably start a few lines down from the top, and the last page of a chapter, which may or may not fill the page). The typing does not have to be absolutely perfect (although standards have risen considerably since the coming of the word processor), and you can be allowed an occasional hand-written correction. But as soon as a page begins to look messy, retype it. If your typescript is a mess, it suggests that you have no pride in your work.

If you are using a word processor, over-ride its prevention of 'widows' (widows occur when the final line of a paragraph appears at the top of the next page without completely filling the line), because you will get some pages which will be a line short if you don't do this.

Do not leave a blank line between paragraphs, unless you want to indicate a change of scene or time or subject, but do indent the first line of each paragraph a few spaces. The style of not indenting paragraphs but leaving a blank line between them is widely used in letters nowadays, but should not be followed for the typescripts of books (or stories or articles, for that matter).

When you produce the final version of your life story, you should number the pages beginning at the first page of the text and going on to the end; don't start with page 1 again with each chapter. As for fastening the typescript together, I would suggest that you should not use pins or paperclips or staples or ring binders, and whatever else you do, don't have it bound into a solid lump. Most publishers prefer a typescript to be in separate sheets, kept together in the wallet type folders which can be found in any stationers (not the plastic folders, which look pretty but are much too slippery).

These rules may all seem rather pernickety, and extravagant too – what with double spacing and good margins, you will use a lot of paper, but paper is comparatively cheap (and paper for typing is mostly made nowadays from replaceable forests). As for all the do's and don't's, there are good reasons for sticking to the rules: it will be easy to make corrections or to add instructions to the book's printer on a typescript produced in this style; it will make your work look more professional; it is what publishers want, and they want it presented in that way because, and this is the most important reason of all, a typescript in this style is easier to read. Besides, you should be aware that if you are going to send your story to a publisher, editors are rarely reluctant to return a book unread if it is presented, for instance, in single spacing, or with masses of handwritten corrections or without margins to the pages.

You may wonder whether, in these computer-controlled days, publishers like to have books submitted to them on disc. We have not yet progressed quite that far, although the time will undoubtedly come when editors will no longer be prepared to read hard copy. So at the moment the answer is 'no', and you should send in a typescript. However, if your book is accepted for publication, the publisher may then ask for a copy on disc (usually on a 3½-inch floppy disc, and often in a special format such as 'Text Only' or 'Rich Text Format'), and it will be used in the production process.

The Prelims

'The prelims' are the first or preliminary pages of a book. They usually consist, in order, of a half-title (simply the title of the book), a list of previous books by the same author, a title page (giving the title, the author's name and the publisher's name), a printing history page (on which is found the copyright notice and statement of moral rights, the date of publication, conditions of sale, and the full imprints of both publisher and printer), and then, if appropriate, pages bearing the dedication, a quotation or two perhaps, a list of contents and list of illustrations. Sometimes, if space is available there will also be a number of blank pages in the prelims, but in other cases more than one item can be put on one page. This depends largely on the number of pages in the complete book; printers work on large sheets of paper, which are then folded to make sections of 32, 16 or 8 pages; if the text of your book occupies, say, 118 pages, and your index takes 2 pages, then there will be 8 pages available for the prelims, making a total of 128 pages.

If the book is accepted by a publisher, the author is expected to supply some of this material, but much of it will be added by the publisher. On the other hand, if you self-publish (see Chapter 10) you will need to prepare all of it. The preliminary material that you will be expected to supply for a publisher would be the assertion of moral rights (see Chapter 8), the dedication, quotations if you want to use them, and the list of contents and illustrations. Your typescript should also have a titlepage, giving the title of the book, your name or pseudonym as the author, and if someone has written an introduction or foreword for you, 'with an introduction (foreword) by A.N. Other'. Your name and full address should appear at the bottom of the page.

The Title

You can call your book anything you like, other than by the title of a book which is already very well known (see

Chapter 8), but it will probably be worth your while to try to find something a little more intriguing than, for instance, 'My Autobiography' or 'The Life of Joe Bloggs' or 'Memoirs'. A title as stark as that might be all right for someone whose name is highly marketable on its own, but although you don't want to go over the top, readers – and publishers' editors – are more likely to pick up a book with an interesting title than one which suggests that the lack of imagination which the author has shown in deciding what to call the book may well apply to its contents too. You might be able to find your title in an appropriate quotation or a phrase which refers in some way to your career or to a recurrent theme in your life. If you are worried that a title of that sort does not give any indication of what the book is actually about, you can always add 'an autobiography' or 'a self-portrait' or 'the story of my life' or something similar as a sub-title. Time spent on finding a good title will not be wasted.

Illustrations

You will remember that Alice, before her adventures in Wonderland, asked what was the use of a book without pictures or conversations. I have already written in Chapter 4 of the value of dialogue (Alice's 'conversations'), and she was right too about pictures, at least as far as many books are concerned, and certainly when it comes to autobiography. Photographs of you at various stages of your life, and of the family and other relations and friends can add a great deal of interest, and to a lesser degree, since people are always more interesting than buildings and scenery and the like, so can views of places which have been important in your life. There may also be drawings of various kinds which would enhance the book, or perhaps reproductions of documents or other papers. The inclusion of any kind of illustration is worthy of consideration, and indeed, a gentleman called Frederick R. Barnard, apparently quoting an ancient Chinese saying, made the accurate observation that 'one picture is worth ten thousand words'.

Your own album and other family archives will probably provide most of the illustrations you need. The important question of copyright may need to be considered, and that subject is covered in Chapter 8, but your first question when you are gathering illustrative material together must be whether the quality of the pictures is satisfactory. Many snapshots taken a long time ago will have faded, or become creased or otherwise damaged, and although cracks and stains can sometimes be removed, it is difficult to restore depth of tone to faded pictures, and they may not reproduce well. Of lesser importance is the fact that not all of us have a good photographer's eye; although many of our snaps have far too much foreground, or the main subject has slipped out of centre or has become tilted, such faults can be easily rectified. In any case, you will probably need to have most of the photographs copied so that they can be enlarged or made smaller or cropped or otherwise altered, because you wiil need to consider what space you want to give each one and how it will fit on the page.

Not all that long ago it was customary for a publisher to group all the photographs in a book together in special sections, printed on a glossier paper than that used for the text. Some books are still produced that way, but the developments in printing, which have resulted in almost all books nowadays being printed from film rather than directly from metallic type, mean that it is simple to place the illustrations at the appropriate places in the text, provided that the quality of paper used is good enough to give a satisfactory reproduction.

This facility also allows you to include as many illustrations as you like, but of course the more you put in, the longer the book will be, and therefore the more expensive to produce. Besides which, you must be careful not to be tempted into including too many pictures which are too similar or of comparatively little interest. If you are hoping that your book will be published by a commercial firm, it may be as well to leave the question of how many illustrations should go in, and how they should be reproduced, until you have succeeded in interesting a publisher in the book. Simply keep the pictures ready for use if need be.

Index

A widely held view is that any non-fiction book should have an index, unless it happens to be some kind of reference book which is already in alphabetical order. Certainly most autobiographies need one (although it is not compulsory), if only so that all your acquaintances, before they read the book as a whole, can look themselves up in the index and turn to the relevant pages first.

The compilation of an index can be a laborious job, demanding the skills of a professional. The Society of Indexers is always willing to suggest one of its members who would be suitable for your book, especially since they have experts in most fields, which may be helpful if your life story contains a certain amount of technical detail. However, the charges will not be slight, and you may well decide to prepare your own index.

There are two main rules to remember. The first, and most important, is that you should always bear in mind the use that the reader is going to make of the index. You could, for instance, index that last sentence as 'Reader's use of index' and the page number, but no one would be likely to look for that in the index. It would be better simply to cover it under 'Index'. In other words, try to put yourself in the reader's mind and work out what things might be looked up, and what would not.

The second rule is that you should not put more than about six page references against any one entry in the index, because it makes it too laborious for the reader to look them all up; it is better to split such multiple entries, where possible, into sub-entries, which will give a more precise indication of the subject matter, so that, for example, if this book had a large number of references to indexes, one might have something like this:

Index, 28, 37, 57, 94, 98, 120
Index, reader's use of, 102
Index, compilation of, 73, 95–6

In the same way, part of the index of your own life might be in this style:

Bloggs, Joe
  birth, 10
  at school, 12–18
  joins Loamshire Bank, 25
  marriage, 28, 47, 90
  becomes Director Loamshire Bank, 73
  retirement, 126–8

You should probably include in the index all the names of those you mention (even if you have been indulging in name-dropping), especially if they are likely to buy the book, but this does not mean that you need to index a name which you have merely casually quoted, as, for example, Mr Barnard, to whom I referred in the first paragraph of the section on illustrations in this chapter.

The preparation of the index cannot be completed until proof stage, when you can insert the correct page numbers, but it is sensible to do as much as you can in advance, especially if your book is accepted by a publisher, because the time at proof stage is often limited. So prepare an index on the basis of your typescript; it is then comparatively easy to find all the references in the printed pages and amend the numbers accordingly.

Family Tree

It may be of great interest to your readers to include a family tree, and it will probably help them to work out who everyone is and what their relationships to each other are. However, this is probably necessary only if you have given a lot of space and attention to your family. If you are not going to mention your forebears more than briefly, and if your family is not a large one, then forget it. If you do want to include a family tree, either prepare it yourself in a form from which it could be reproduced, remembering that it will have to fit on to a page or two facing pages of the book (which is greatly preferable to having one of those huge sheets of folded paper which have to be pulled out from the book, and can easily become unstuck), or write it out roughly so that someone else can do it neatly and in a professional style, which will be much simpler for you.

Footnotes

Footnotes are generally a pain. They are usually set in a smaller type than the main text, and their insertion often causes havoc with the paging of the text. This is why you will often find all the footnotes lumped together at the end of a chapter or at the end of the book (publishers vary in their preferences in this matter). Of course, if you are preparing camera-ready copy on your computer (for which you will require some expertise – see Chapter 10) you can put in as many footnotes as you like and in any style you like, for it is only you who will have the problem of working them out. In most cases it is much better, if you can possibly manage it, to include in the main text whatever information it may be, rather than using footnotes.

Acknowledgements

If you have used any material the copyright of which belongs to someone else, you will have to obtain permission for its inclusion and give the relevant details in a formal acknowledgement (see Chapter 8). You may also wish to thank various people for help, or to acknowledge the fact that, in the course of writing your story, you have consulted a great many books. The three things are rather different, and might appear as three separate lists under 'Acknowledgements', 'Thanks' and 'Bibliography'. Alternatively, they could appear on the same page under the heading 'Acknowledgements', although probably in separate sections. It is more usual to keep the Bibliography separate, but the Acknowledgements and Thanks are often combined. The wording when you are acknowledging permission to quote from copyright work will have to follow the style dictated by the copyright owner, the thanks can be phrased in any way that you prefer, and the list of books will need to give details of author, publisher and date of publication.

It is entirely a matter of choice whether you put the

acknowledgements at the beginning of the book in the prelims or at the end, although bibliographies are usually at the back of the book.

8 Your Rights and Those of Others

Copyright

Everything that you write or record on tape or disc is copyright as soon as it exists (provided, of course, that it is original to you, and is not just a copy of someone else's work). The copyright belongs to you, and it lasts for seventy years after death or first publication, whichever is the later, so that you can leave it in your will for the benefit of your heirs. You don't need to register your copyright, or even to state on the original typescript of whatever piece of work it may be that the copyright is yours (although it does no harm and may in some circumstances be helpful to use the formula 'Copyright © Joe Bloggs 1999', the date being the year of publication or of completion). If a reputable publisher takes your book, someone in the firm will ensure that a copyright notice appears in all copies of the book – you will be able to see it in this book on the reverse of the title page. It pays publishers to have the protection that this gives against anyone else using the material without permission and without paying. If you have any doubts about whether your publisher is reputable or whether perhaps the firm is so small and new that it might not know the rules, then check at proof stage to see that the copyright notice (usually printed on the reverse of the title page) is properly stated in your name. But you should have no trouble.

If you publish the book yourself you should certainly ensure that a copyright notice, using the formula given in the paragraph above, is printed in all copies of the book.

Never surrender your copyright. If your book is accepted for publication you will normally be expected to grant the publishers a licence covering the volume rights, allowing them to produce the work in book form, and often giving them control of and the ability to sell various subsidiary rights, splitting moneys received from the latter in agreed proportions (details of the rights which may be licensed to publishers and the acceptable splits of income are to be found in the Minimum Terms Agreement printed in my book *An Author's Guide to Publishing*, published by Robert Hale). But you do *not* grant them the copyright. Nor, despite a myth prevalent in some writers' circles which says that you should put the letters 'F.B.S.R.' on everything you write, do you offer a publisher First British Serial Rights in your book. You grant First British Serial Rights to a magazine or newspaper when you sell them a short story or article, but you retain the copyright. In fact, there is no need to give any indication on the typescript of a book as to which rights you are offering – publishers will assume that, if they wish to publish the book, you will grant them the volume rights, and details of the territories in which they will be able to exercise their licence and of which subsidiary rights they will control will all be sorted out at contract stage.

If you publish the book yourself, make sure that no one else, such as the printer, claims copyright in it, except perhaps a joint author.

There is no copyright in ideas. Because this is so, some authors worry a great deal about the possibility that a publisher to whom they have submitted a proposal will reject the idea, and then pinch it and then get someone else to write the book. Reputable publishers do not indulge in such tricks. The scare stories that you hear are usually the result of coincidence rather than malpractice by an unscrupulous publisher. In any case, the problem is hardly likely to affect the author of an autobiography.

You may, however, need to be careful about the title of your book, because, although there is no copyright in titles either, you could be sued for 'passing off' if you have chosen a title which is already famous. 'Passing off' means using a well-known title in order to persuade the public to buy your book in the belief that it is the celebrated one.

Moral Rights

One of the good things to come out of the EU has been the harmonization of copyright practices among member states. Britain's response to the EU directive was the Copyright, Designs and Patents Act of 1988, which, among a great many other matters, recognized the Moral Rights owned by the creators of artistic material, which include authors. The Act defines four Moral Rights.

The two principal Moral Rights are usually known as 'The Right of Paternity' and 'The Right of Integrity'. The former ensures that the author's origination of the material will be acknowledged in any publication of it, in any medium and whether in whole or in part. The latter protects the author from any unauthorized mutilation or distortion of the material in an adaptation or other treatments of it.

The other two Moral Rights are of lesser importance, one preventing the attribution to an author of work by someone else, while the other prevents the publication without permission of photographs or film which have been taken for private or domestic use.

The two Moral Rights described in the paragraph above and the Right of Integrity all exist and operate without the need for any action on the part of the author. The Right of Paternity, however, requires to be 'asserted', and your typescript should therefore include a page in the prelims on which you type: 'The right of Joe Bloggs (or Joan Bloggs or whatever your name is) to be identified as the author of this work has been asserted by him (or her) in accordance with the Copyright, Designs and Patents Act 1988'. And you should check that the notice appears in the prelims of the printed book – again you will be able to see the assertion in respect of this book on the reverse of the title page.

Public Lending Right

If your book is commercially published the publisher will hope to sell copies to the Public Libraries; if you self-publish you may be able to get copies into the libraries, as described in Chapter 10. Once your book is available for borrowing you can register for Public Lending Right, by writing to Public Lending Right Office, Bayheath House, Prince Regent Street, Stockton-on-Tees, Cleveland TS18 1DF. If your book is taken out of libraries frequently enough you will receive PLR payment. Your Public Lending Right belongs exclusively to you, so you do not have to share it with a publisher or printer or anyone else, other than perhaps a joint author.

Using Copyright Material

The laws of copyright apply to everyone, and are in effect throughout most of the world, so if you quote from someone else's work you will be infringing their copyright unless the author concerned has been dead for more than seventy years, or unless you seek permission to use the quotation. The only real freedom to quote without permission comes under the heading of 'fair dealing', an arrangement enshrined in the 1988 Copyright, Designs and Patents Act, which allows the use of quoted material for the purpose of review or criticism. This is not likely to have much application to an autobiography, but if you do wish to invoke 'fair dealing', you should know that, although the Act does not define how much material can be quoted, an agreement between the Society of Authors and the Publishers Association allows the quotation of a passage of up to 400 words or 40 lines of a poem (provided that the lines used are not more than a quarter of the whole poem) without permission. Publishers are sometimes liberal in their interpretation of the stricture that the material can be used freely only in the course of 'review or criticism', but you should always check the position and seek permission for any quotations. It is easier and safer to quote only from authors who are out of copyright. And in every case of a copyright extract you will need to indicate in your book the name of the work from which you quote, its author and its publisher; these details can either be incorporated into your text at the point where you are using the material, or (as is usually more convenient) listed on a page in the prelims.

In order to obtain permission to quote copyright material you should write to the publisher of the work which you want to use, giving full details of the passage concerned, and of the use that you are going to make of it. When granting you permission, the publisher will normally tell you the form in which the acknowledgement should be made. You may have to pay a fee, and supply a copy of your book, and the more eminent the author you are quoting, the higher the fee. Poetry will probably cost more than prose, and among the most expensive material to quote is the lyrics of popular songs. Very often the fee quoted for anything that you want to use will be so high that it will be wiser not to include the material at all – some copyright owners are excessively greedy.

Since those who give you permission to quote from works which they control usually expect reasonably prompt payment, it is advisable not to apply for any permission until you are certain that the book is going to be published, whether by a commercial firm or by you yourself. Besides, if the book is to be commercially published, the publisher may wish you to obtain any permissions for world-wide use, rather than simply for British territories, and will advise you accordingly.

All the above also applies, of course, to illustrations, with the added complication that if you want to use a painting which is in one of the national collections, you will have to pay a fee despite the fact that the artist may have been dead for far more than seventy years.

If you are desperately eager to use material which you know must be in copyright, but the owner of which you have failed to trace despite many attempts, put a notice in your book to that effect, asking the copyright owner to contact you to regularize the position. You should keep, as evidence that you have tried, copies of any letters you have written in your attempts to solve the problem.

Don't think that if you are self-publishing the book and printing a few copies only for close friends and relatives, so that in effect it is a private edition, there will be no need to clear quoted material; even if you give a full acknowledgement of the source of the material, what you are doing still amounts to publication, and the use of the quotations in your book without permission will be an infringement of their authors' copyright, and you could be sued.

Even worse than trying to get away with it on the

grounds of private use, is the idea of not acknowledging where the material comes from and passing it off as your own work. It seems to me unlikely to be something that would happen to any great extent in an autobiography, but if it did, it would be what is called 'plagiarism'. 'Plagiarism' is just another word for 'stealing', and is just as much a crime.

It may not surprise you that anything printed in a book is likely to be in copyright, but it sometimes comes as a shock to learn that the copyright in letters which you have in your possession does not belong to you. The physical letter – the paper and the ink or pencil marks on it – is yours and you may do whatever you like with it, but the wording of the letter is the copyright of the person who wrote it, and remains so, unless the writer grants it to someone else, until seventy years after his or her death. So you will need to get permission if you want to quote a letter which was written to you, and I would suggest that you should do so even if the copyright owner is very close to you and unlikely to be upset at what you are doing. Relationships can change.

Photographs, too, can prove difficult. Until the 1988 Act, photographs taken at the behest of the sitter were the sitter's copyright. Nowadays, however, the copyright belongs to the photographer, even if you have dictated exactly what the photographs are to be and have paid for them to be taken. However, it may be possible to overcome the problem if the photographer is willing to sell the copyright.

Libel

The important thing to be remembered about libel, which can be very damaging to its perpetrators, is that it does not exist unless you say something deleterious about someone else – something which will damage their reputation or, even worse, their livelihood. I have suggested earlier in this book that you may have to avoid anything which will upset your friends or relatives; that is a matter of choice. In contrast, it is essential to avoid libel, because it will almost certainly mean a very expensive court case, and probably the destruction of all copies of your book.

There are four principal defences to an accusation of libel: the first is that the material complained of is true (which is fine, except that it may be very difficult to prove it); the second is that of 'fair comment' (and you would have to prove that what you wrote was a matter of opinion and not activated by malice on your part); the third is that of 'privilege' (which applies to reports of judicial or parliamentary proceedings); and the fourth is that of 'innocence' (in which you claim that you did not even know of the plaintiff's existence – which is hardly likely to apply in the case of libel in an autobiography).

Don't believe for a moment that you will get away with libellous material by not naming the persons concerned or trying to disguise them in some way. As long as any of their friends or acquaintances can recognize them, they will have a case against you. The only let-off you have is that you cannot libel the dead, but you still have to be careful that what you say about anyone who has fallen off the twig is not damaging to the descendants of that person, who would then be able to sue.

You may think that your book will not be subject to the dangers of libel if you produce a few copies only for private circulation among your relatives and close friends. Wrong. That still counts legally as publication, so the situation is the same as already cited in the matter of using copyright material without permission.

Obscenity, Blasphemy, Sedition and Other Offensive Material

Authors used to have to be very careful not to offend against all sorts of taboos. Nowadays, you can say just about anything you want without fear of your book being banned or prosecuted. That applies particularly to blow-by-blow accounts of sexual encounters and to the so-called 'four-letter words', which seem to form a large part of most published books nowadays – at least, of the fiction. Don't, however, be misled into believing that your book will not interest a publisher unless it is full of that kind of material. It isn't true, and in any case, it is best to write in your own natural style, and to please yourself and the kind of people that you hope will read the book.

It should be pointed out, on the other hand, that the betrayal of state secrets is still an offence, and if your life has involved working on highly confidential matters, whether these have been connected with the secret services or the military, you will probably need to clear your book with the authorities before going ahead. Equally, you could find yourself in trouble if you reveal too many industrial secrets.

9 Professional Assistance

Ghost Writers

It may be that after reading what I have said earlier in this book you have decided that writing your own story is a bit too difficult. I should like to persuade you that you are wrong, and at least to have a shot at it, because, if you persevere, you will probably find it both easier and more enjoyable than you think. But words may not come readily to you, even if you try using some kind of recording device so that you don't have to put anything on paper and need not worry about spelling and punctuation (although you will have to find a secretary to transcribe your material). If so, you may be wondering about getting someone else to write your book – a ghost writer, perhaps. Ghost writers are often called in to undertake the autobiographies of eminent people, who either have no time or, more often, feel (or their publishers feel) that they do not have the ability to write effectively.

How does a ghost work? First of all, by meeting the subject of the book and discovering whether the two of them will be able work together reasonably happily. A ghost is a professional and is therefore usually willing to write someone's life story (provided the pay is right) whether or not the person concerned is likeable or admirable. Ghost writers are used to suppressing their personal feelings, although in some cases they may refuse an assignment because they feel the client or the story is just too unpleasant, or perhaps because they are not in sympathy with the celebrity's views on politics or some other major issue. But it is essential that ghost and protagonist should be able to talk freely to each other, and this demands a certain empathy between them. Above all, the ghost must inspire trust in the subject, because their relationship will be in some ways rather like that of a Roman Catholic priest hearing the confession of one of his parishioners – the person whose life story is to be told must be willing to reveal all manner of secrets, relying on the ghost's promise not to use anything deleterious.

Having decided that they can produce a book together, and when terms have been agreed (a subject to which we shall return later), the ghost sets about gathering material for the book. This usually involves spending several days or weeks with the subject, asking questions, jogging the memory, finding out everything possible. The ghost will dig really deeply, as already suggested, persuading the 'victim' to strip away as many veils as possible. Their conversations will be recorded on tape (it is usual for the ghost to sign a declaration that the recordings will not be used for any purpose other than that of writing the proposed book, and will be destroyed thereafter). The ghost may also have to do quite a lot of detailed research to fill in the background of the story. The ghost will play the tapes of the conversations with the subject over and over again, not merely in order to extract the facts of the person's life, but to capture the tone, the phrasing, the vocabulary which he or she uses. Ghost writers are like actors, assuming the personality of the client whose story they are writing, and this is why, with autobiographies produced by really capable ghosts, it is always easy to believe that they were written by the subjects themselves.

When the book is finished, the ghost writer usually has a major hurdle to negotiate because the subject has to agree the text before it is printed. There is often some disagreement, because people rarely have a balanced view of themselves, especially if they are celebrities, used to projecting an image of themselves which may not be a true reflection of their personalities.

So, how do you set about finding a ghost to write your autobiography? Well, you probably don't, unless you have some fame, or even notoriety, in which case you will have been approached in the first place by a publisher, who will arrange matters as far as the ghost is concerned. If you are not famous, you are unlikely to interest the professionals sufficiently for any of them to take the task on. And the reason for this is that they make their livings this way – they don't work 'on spec'. They want to know that the book will be published in due course, and that they will be paid for writing it (the arrangement is usually that all royalties from the book are split between the subject and the ghost – most often 50/50). What is more they need to have money up front, because they have to live and keep their families while the writing is in progress, and may have to pay the not inconsiderable expenses incurred if, for example, a lot of travel, with accompanying hotel bills, is involved. For this reason they will usually not commit themselves to working on a ghosted autobiography unless a publisher has already signed the proposed book up.

There is rarely any problem in interesting a ghost if the client is someone in the public eye, but anyone else will find it rather more difficult without having a publishing agreement in hand. If you are wealthy enough to pay a ghost on such 'on spec' terms, it would probably be possible to find one (you might advertise in the magazines for writers, such as *Writers News* and *Writers' Forum*), but the cost would be substantial – probably in the region of £5,000, plus fairly hefty expenses – and there would be no guarantee at all of any quality or even of integrity, so you would need to check anyone who came forward very thoroughly. It is unlikely that one of the well-established, highly capable ghosts would be tempted, because the professionals in this field do not rely solely on the initial fees they receive. They want to be sure that any book which they take on is going to be commercially and successfully published, because only then can they hope seriously for additional payments to come in when the book is paperbacked or published in the United States or translated and published in non-English-speaking countries.

One other possibility which would relieve the financial problems would be to find a willing relative or friend to ghost your story for you without payment, or for a token sum only, at least until the book was commercially published. You would need to assure yourself in advance of the ghost's ability to put words together effectively, so that the book would be readable, and you should also feel confident that you could trust the writer to tell your story as you want it told.

If you were to come to some arrangement with one of what I will call the '£5,000 ghosts' mentioned above, or with a friend or relative, it would be very important to draw up an agreement specifying your rights and how any moneys which might arise from publication or any other use should be split between you. I would suggest that in either case the copyright should be held exclusively by you, even if for you to own it outright would seem rather unfair to the ghost, and you should have sole control of any use to be made of the material. As for any income, the '£5,000 ghost' should not get any additional sums – the money is a flat fee – but you might consider giving your friend or relative a small share.

If you use a ghost your name will still appear as the

apparent author of the book, but the ghost will be given credit under the legend 'as told to' or even more succinctly 'with'. Some people feel that the fact that the book has been written by someone other than the subject is reprehensible – a form of cheating, even when it is made clear that the supposed autobiographer received substantial help. In fact, as long as the help is clearly acknowledged, what the reader has is a genuine autobiography, based entirely on the facts supplied by the person whose story it is, and probably much more capably and entertainingly written than would have been the case if he or she had done the job without assistance.

Collaboration

It may be that you do not really want a ghost writer, but would certainly like some help with the writing, perhaps to organize the way the story is told, and to polish up the prose, without necessarily writing every word as a ghost would do – a collaborator, in fact, by which term I mean someone who works with the autobiographer on the text of the book, whereas a ghost takes information only from the subject and is entirely responsible for the writing. Again, you may have a member of the family who would be prepared to collaborate, but in some respects that might be rather like being taught to drive by your nearest and dearest – liable to produce arguments and ill-feeling. It rather depends on whether the working relationship which you decided upon would be similar to that of a boss and secretary, or whether it would be a matter of a complete partnership.

Depending on circumstances, of course, collaboration might work very well, especially if your collaborator can contribute substantially to the content of the book. Some professional writing collaborations take the form of the two partners sitting down together and bouncing ideas off each other so that it would be very difficult to say which of them was responsible for this or that part of the final script, but this is really more appropriate for something like radio or television scripts in which fleeting images and jokes are required. In other cases, one partner provides the basic ideas, and the other fleshes them out. But with very few exceptions, collaborations seem to work best when, however much discussion may go on, the actual writing is done by one person working on his/her own, but then allowing the other collaborator to suggest changes. The exception to this is when different chapters are written by the subject and the assistant because each has knowledge of certain happenings in a more complete form than the other. This could be a good working method for partners, one of whom might be concerned, for instance, with the business side of their lives, and the other with a more domestic view. The main thing, however, is to decide in advance what each collaborator will do, and will not do – lay down the parameters and there is far less likelihood of disagreements later, and you will avoid the embarrassment of help and advice turning into interference. If your collaborator is a friend, rather than a member of the family, that will probably make things easier, because politeness will ensure that you are less likely to be over-critical or to fly off the handle, but this does not obviate the need to agree on procedures before you start work together.

Professional Editors

Professional editorial assistance is also available, and that too can be as extensive or as limited as you wish, although it is unlikely to stretch quite as far as total collaboration.

The help would probably be restricted to detailed and constructive comments on how to improve the quality and interest of the writing, but could involve an almost complete re-writing job. Any of the magazines for writers, such as *Writers' Forum* or *Writers News*, usually carry a number of small ads inserted by professional freelance editors. Naturally you would have to pay, and the costs would depend on the length of your book and the amount of work needed – most such editors charge on an hourly basis. They are not cheap, but neither are they excessively costly, and considering the level of their skills, cannot be considered to be over-priced.

If you are inclined to think that the charges are on the steep side, you might consider the fact that these professional freelances are probably the only people you could go to in order to get an unbiased and honest opinion of your book, and that could be worth a great deal to you. On the whole, they like to encourage rather than to be overly critical, feeling that it is not within their remit to destroy utterly the self-confidence of the author, the pleasure that has been gained from writing the book, and his/her hopes for its future. For this reason it is often true that the harsher the comments of such editors, the better the book, whereas they will be much more gentle in pointing out the book's faults and offering suggestions for its improvement when dealing with a talentless author. If you were to say, however, that you wanted a totally honest opinion, however brutal it might be, making it clear that you really would prefer to be told, if that is the case, that the book was hopeless and should be abandoned, you would almost certainly get it, or something approaching it. But don't ask for that kind of verdict unless you are prepared for the worst, and ready to accept what the editor says. Not all editors are good at recognizing a good book (which is why some eventual best-sellers have had a hard time at first in finding a publisher), but almost all of them are infallible when it comes to sniffing out something useless. On the other hand, of course, the more honest the negative opinions are, the more likely it is that the nuggets of praise will be entirely genuinely meant.

10 Getting Into Print

Commercial Publishers

Disappointing although it may be, it must be made clear at the outset of this chapter that you have very little chance of getting your autobiography published by a commercial publisher unless you are famous. There are two or three slightly encouraging possibilities which we will come to later, but by and large you haven't much hope, when you send your book off to a publisher, of getting a six-figure offer for the rights by return, or even of receiving an advance payment of the meanest proportions after long weeks of waiting and from the twenty-seventh firm to which you have shown the work. Don't despair, however, because there are other alternatives available, and these, too will be discussed later in this chapter.

First, however, let us look at the reason that it is so difficult to get an autobiography into print. The problem is simply one of how the publisher will be able to sell the book if you are unknown to readers at large – how it will be possible to persuade booksellers to order it, and libraries to stock it, and the general public to buy or borrow it. You need to have a name which is familiar to a very substantial number of potential readers outside your relatives and personal friends. If you go into a bookshop and look at the new autobiographies, you might see one by Berengaria (or Marmaduke) Thingumme, of whom you have never heard, in among others by people whose names are household words; it is possible – just – that you will pick up the Thingumme book, but unless the blurb is very enticing, you will almost certainly put it down again fairly rapidly, and buy a book about someone whose name you know and whose background is of interest to you. The same is true if you go to a library – on the whole, your eye is likely to skim past an autobiography by an unknown, never mind the fact that it may be a lot more interesting than the memoirs of some sports or pop star with an IQ of practically nothing and whose life has lasted barely a couple of decades. Even if you have an exceptionally wide circle of friends and relatives, you will have a hard time convincing a publisher that a large enough market can found from them. Most publishers are well aware that the hundreds of friends and relatives who authors swear will buy the book are made up mostly of people who will either neglect to do so or will borrow a copy which has already been read by a dozen of the author's other buddies.

You needn't think, by the way, that publication will itself make you famous; unless your book is of really outstanding quality, your publisher is unlikely to spend a fortune on promoting it, it will be ignored by the national press, and your invitation to appear on a TV chat-show will never arrive.

There are exceptions to the rule that your name has to be instantly recognizable. For a start, we might consider degrees of fame. It is one thing if you are a familiar and major star, but it is quite possible to be almost unknown to the public at large and yet to be very eminent in your own particular field. I would be surprised if one person in a hundred would recognize the name of, let us say, the president of one of the City Guilds, but such a person has almost certainly had an exceptional career, is very highly thought of within that trade, and the trade itself is large enough to guarantee a lot of people for whom his autobiography would be required reading. Moreover, the office of president will undoubtedly have brought its holder into contact with opposite numbers in other trades, and a wide circle of friends and acquaintances really will be eager to read the story (and at that level of success you buy books – you don't borrow them).

Another possibility is that the author's life is of quite exceptional interest. Perhaps you have done a variety of genuinely exciting jobs in various parts of the world, or you might be an unsung heroine, or you could have been a behind-the-scenes observer at events of international importance over a period of many years. We live in an age in which the media are always hungry for new stories and new personalities, and most real-life characters such as I have just mentioned are more than likely to have been discovered and presented to the Great British Public, and have already become famous. But there are still men and women who have always kept themselves private, until perhaps in later life they decide to tell their stories in the form of an autobiography, and if you are such a person, then indeed you have a chance of commercial publication.

Then there are those who have already been mentioned several times in this book – the literary autobiographers, the poets, the writers whose prose is of such high quality that the way they tell the story of their lives, with a great deal of charm as well as the beautiful writing, is at least as important as their content. Every publisher in the world is looking for a new Laurie Lee.

Another possibility is the so-called 'nostalgia' books. These are almost always autobiographies which are solely concerned with the author's childhood, and to be successful they usually go back fifty or sixty years from the period in which they are written, so that at present a childhood spent in the 1930s or 40s would be acceptable. The other thing which their authors need is almost total recall (or an enormous amount of research) because the books depend for their effect largely on the mass of detail which readers of the same age will enjoy being reminded of. You should be able to remember how much it cost on the tram from here to there, and how many milk jujubes you could get for a halfpenny, and what they tasted like, and how much you hated the scratchy woollen underclothes that you were forced to wear in winter, and the way your grandmother dressed, and so on. What is more, you must be able to link all this material together in a book which has some shape to it, and an underlying content, beyond a mere list of memories, which will keep the reader interested.

Yet another kind of autobiography which can still find a publisher is the anecdotal or humorous book, of which perhaps the James Herriot titles and Richard Gordon's doctor stories are a good example, but these usually have a considerable degree of fiction mixed in (as was true of both Herriot's and Gordon's bestsellers). There is normally no attempt in such books to cover the author's entire life – you simply select a few amusing or interesting episodes. You also need to have quite a degree of originality; it would help, for instance, if you were to write about a trade or business which has not already been covered in this way in a series of books, and such backgrounds are pretty rare nowadays. It is not easy in any case to write humorous material successfully, and it is even more difficult to get it published because you have to find an editor who has the same sense of humour as your own. If you are tempted into this kind of writing, please don't try to write a comic book about your experience in moving house – in basic terms everyone finds moving either very funny or so awful that it develops into absurdity, and publishers' editors find such books very tiresome because they are all the same and in almost every case the incidents are far less amusing than the author thinks.

Submitting Your Work to a Publisher

Authors of non-fiction books, which of course include autobiographies, have a great advantage over novelists in that it is seldom necessary to write a complete book before discovering whether or not a publisher would be interested in taking it on. There are many reasons, explained in Chapter 1, why you should write your life-story anyway, but if you are interested in being professionally published and think you have a chance of reaching that goal, then you can approach a publisher at a very early stage.

You need first to do a little market research to discover which publishers might be interested in your book. Go to libraries and bookshops to check on this question, asking advice too; librarians are always helpful, and bookshop owners and managers, like anyone else, are usually delighted to talk about something in which they are expert, provided of course that you do not choose their busiest time to ask your questions. You would probably find the big spring and autumn numbers of *The Bookseller* (the organ of the book trade) of interest, and both booksellers and libraries are likely to have copies on file, which they would probably allow you to consult; these special numbers contain advertisements from all the leading publishing houses, giving details of their forthcoming books, and their listings can give you a good idea of what kind of books are likely to appeal to them.

When you have done some research of this nature, you should end up with a list of possible publishers. Make it a long list, if you can, because you may need it. Now check the names on your list against the information given in *Writers' and Artists' Yearbook* or *The Writer's Handbook* (both available in libraries) and cross off any of those publishers which are indicated as being unwilling to accept submissions direct from members of the public, preferring to consider only those books which come to them via an agent. Then telephone those of the remaining publishers which seem the most likely bets, and find out the name of an editor who deals with non-fiction, so that you can write to that editor by name.

Write a brief, business-like letter and enclose a succinct summary of your book (that is to say, the main points of your life), making it sound as interesting as you can, and give some idea of the length you expect the finished work to be. (If you are going to self-publish your life story – a subject to which we shall return later – it does not matter how long or short your book is, but a commercial publisher will not normally be interested in anything less than 50,000 or more than 120,000 words.) You should also give details of the number of illustrations you would like to see included, and whether you contemplate an index or a bibliography or any other such material. It is not advisable to send the illustrations at this stage, but it might be worth including a list of them. As for the synopsis, if you have prepared a detailed plan for yourself, as suggested in Chapter 2, you may be able to shorten it (a publisher won't need or want all the detail that you might have included for your own purposes) to occupy something like a couple of typed pages, and it should be accompanied by one or two specimen chapters. I would suggest that the latter should always include the first chapter, and should probably go on with chapters two and three, but if you prefer to send those sections of the book which tell the most exciting parts of your story, then there is no reason why you should not do so (but do try to make sure that they really are exciting –

otherwise the publisher is likely to think that if those are the best bits of the book, the rest must be pretty boring). The synopsis tells the publisher what the content of the book will be, and the specimen chapters are there to prove that you can write not merely competently, but well enough to keep a reader interested.

You should also try to give some idea of the kind of market that you think would exist for the book, especially if you can say that you belong to some organization the members of which could be mailed with publicity for the book. It sometimes happens that an author can actually guarantee the sale of a given number of copies of a book to some such society, and the publisher will always be interested in such information, especially if the quantity involved is substantial. This is also the occasion to reveal, if it is so, that you could get a foreword for your book from a person of some fame or eminence. Anything which will indicate why your book will stand out from the herd, what angles could be used in promoting it, what particular value it has – such matters should always be included to tempt the publisher. But don't expect to excite much interest by suggesting that all your relations, friends and acquaintance will buy copies – as already mentioned, publishers are rightly sceptical about such claims. Above all, don't include the information that your relatives and friends all think the book is wonderful – the publisher knows very well that they are unlikely to have said anything else, even if they were bored to tears.

Some publishers can be tempted if you offer to subsidize them against loss on your book by making an up-front contribution to the costs. This is not the same as vanity publishing (see pages 136–8), partly because reputable publishers would not accept such an offer if they felt the work fell below their normal standards, and partly because you could expect the return of your money, or part of it, if the book were a success. On the whole, the major houses are unlikely to be interested in such a deal, but new small firms might listen favourably to the suggestion.

Always include postage for the return of your material. If, because you use a word processor and can easily run off another copy, you don't need to have the pages back, then make that clear, and at least enclose a stamped addressed envelope for the publisher's reply. If you do not have a computer with the material on disc, always make sure that you retain a copy of the typescript – publishers rarely lose material sent to them, but it does happen on occasion.

Rejection

After you have sent your synopsis and chapters to a publisher you should prepare yourself for the likelihood that the book will be rejected, not necessarily because it isn't very good, but for the reasons explained earlier concerning the publisher's difficulty in selling a book by an unknown author. You must also be patient; the material may come back to you very quickly, but it is much more likely to be several weeks before you hear any news, and the delay is the result not only of the large number of submissions that all publishers receive, which take time to consider, but also because projects which arrive on an editor's desk out of the blue from unknown authors receive a low priority. If the book is rejected, then try the next publisher on your list. A better idea may be to send the material in the first place to several publishers simultaneously. There is nothing to stop you doing this, apart perhaps from the cost of postage, and it is a ploy which publishers accept, although it is courteous to tell the firms concerned that you are submitting your work elsewhere at the same time.

How long should you continue trying to interest publishers without success? It is inadvisable to give up too soon, provided that you are really confident that your book is interesting and original enough and has a reachable market. Many writers have had to persevere through countless rejections before finding a publisher, and achieving a highly successful publication. On the other hand, if you receive nothing but formal rejection slips or letters, without any word of encouragement, from a whole series of publishers, it may be sensible to stop wasting money on postage and look for other possibilities. Incidentally, don't be surprised if you are not given any explanation of why your book has been sent back to you – editors really are busy people, and have quite a job to keep abreast of their work on books which they *are* going to publish, and little time to spare for those which they are not. But if you do get a letter which is complimentary about some aspect of your work, then believe it and be encouraged – publishers don't write that sort of thing unless they mean it. And when editors suggest, as they sometimes do, that the book should be submitted to another publisher, this is a genuine effort to be helpful.

Agents

Literary agents can be of immense use to authors in a great many ways. If you are interested you will find a considerable amount of information on the subject in my book *An Author's Guide to Literary Agents* (published by Hale). However, unless you have an assured market (which means either being famous or at least being prominent in a wide if specialized field) you will probably find it much more difficult to get an agent than to interest a publisher. This is perhaps understandable when you realize that the average first book by an unknown author will not bring its author a sizeable amount of money – and that applies particularly to autobiographies by comparative or complete unknowns – and the agent gets only a small percentage of what the author earns.

The most sensible advice for a first-time writer of any kind is to forget about trying to persuade an agent to take you on. There are still plenty of publishers who are willing to consider work submitted directly by the author – indeed, they outnumber those who will deal only with agents. And if you feel that you really need an agent to guide you through the complexities of the publisher's agreement, the process of publication, royalty statements, subsidiary rights and the like, it will probably be easy enough to find one once you have received an offer from a publisher.

If a Publisher Makes an Offer

If a publisher makes an offer to publish your book, you will probably receive first a letter which will suggest the sum that they will pay as an advance on account of the moneys that the book will earn for you, which will be primarily in the form of royalties. When you happily reply accepting the offer, a formal contract will follow. At this stage, unless you have an agent, one of whose jobs it is to approve the agreement and make sure that it is fair to you, you will need advice. Publishers' contracts are very complex documents, and are likely to be baffling to the layman, and although no reputable publishers cheat – they wouldn't be reputable if they did, and in any case it wouldn't pay them to do so – there may be clauses in the agreement which are less than fair, or which need clarification. Don't be afraid to query anything which you don't like or don't understand. As long as you remain polite, the publisher will not withdraw the offer just because you ask a few questions. But you do need to know what to question, what to object to. The cheapest way to protect yourself is by getting hold of a copy of my book *An Author's Guide to Publishing* (published by Hale), which will probably be useful to you in other matters too, but which I am recommending now because it contains a copy of a Minimum Terms Agreement, which will give you something against which to measure the contract which your publisher has sent you. Better still, although it will cost rather more, is to join the Society of Authors, which you are entitled to do as soon as a commercial publisher has made an offer to publish a book which you have written. The advantages of membership are many, and they include a service which vets publishers' contracts and advises the authors concerned about which clauses they should query or object to, or even fight to get altered.

One thing which you may find very disappointing is that the terms which the publisher offers do not immediately suggest that you should go out and buy yourself a mansion set in a thousand acres, or a Porsche, or even half a dozen bottles of champagne. Unless you get into the bestseller class, or something very near it, the financial rewards for an author are likely to be minimal and to bear little relationship to the amount of work involved in writing the book. If the book is sufficiently interesting to have a large market, it may be published in paperback as well as in hardcover editions, and may sell in the United States and to foreign language publishers, and in that case you will do pretty well – you would at least be able to afford the champagne. It is more likely, however, that you will see little money beyond the advance, and perhaps, if your publisher manages to sell copies to the public libraries, a few pounds from Public Lending Right (payments funded by the Government to reward authors with a token amount each time their books are borrowed). Still, the mere writing of the book is usually a big reward for the author, and seeing it in print gives even more pleasure, so perhaps the financial returns are not all that important.

Self-publishing

If you fail to find a publisher for your work, or indeed if you are realistic enough to decide in the first place that it isn't worth trying to interest a commercial firm in taking you on, then you should certainly consider self-publishing. At one time a certain stigma was attached to self-published books, because they seemed to be announcing to the world that they weren't good enough to attract proper publishers, but their authors were vain enough – and could afford – to bring them out themselves. Nowadays that is no longer so. Because publishers find it much more difficult than in the past to produce books with a limited market and print run, self-publishing has flourished and become respectable, and many self-published books have sold in reasonable quantities and some have had to be reprinted several times.

How do you set about self-publishing your autobiography? You can turn to Yellow Pages and look for local printers, many of whom are equipped to produce small editions of books, and will quote for various quantities. If you are lucky, you may find one which will be prepared to help you with the design of the book and its cover, and even over such matters as copyright and ISBNs (the world-wide system for identifying individual books through a code of numbers). It is always worth shopping around, but, as with most things, you should consider carefully whether the cheapest price will really be an economy in terms of the quality of the finished product and the efficiency with which the firm operates. You will of course have to pay the cost of setting the book in type, the paper, the printing, the binding, and various sundries, plus the printer's profit. The total cost will naturally vary according to the length of the book, and such factors as the number and nature of the illustrations to be included, whether the jacket or cover will be a full colour photograph or something much simpler, and so on, and whether you present the material to the printer in a handwritten manuscript or in typescript form, or on disc. The unit cost will depend also on the quantity printed. If you are thinking in terms of a hundred or two hundred copies, the price per copy may horrify you; if you print more, the figure will drop, and the larger the print quantity the more dramatic the fall. However, you would be well advised to be very pessimistic about the number of copies that you believe you will be able to sell, and you should therefore print the minimum quantity that makes economic sense. You can always reprint if you sell out (and if a large enough unsatisfied demand still exists).

As an alternative to going to a printer, there are now many small firms which will do the whole job for you, finding and negotiating with a printer, designing the book and advising you on all aspects of publication, including the vital point of the retail price which you should put on the book (which should be at least twice the total unit cost, to allow for the discounts you will have to give to any bookshops where it is sold). This service costs a little more than going direct to a printer, but the additional expertise may well be worth it. Such firms advertise regularly in magazines for writers such as *Writers News* and *Writer's Forum*. Again, it is sensible to get quotations from several concerns before making up your mind.

One way of saving quite a lot of the cost is to present a printer with camera-ready copy, an option which is really open only to those who have a computer. All book printing nowadays involves a photographic process, and what you need to do is to present your work exactly as it would appear in a finished book – that is to say, with the text on each page occupying an area of something like 10 cm × 17 cm, with page numbers inserted and running heads (the title of the book and/or the chapter at the top of the page) and all the illustrations in the correct size and place. It is a job for someone who is comparatively expert with the word processor and who has a sense of book design. If that is not you, then forget it.

Whether you go direct to a printer or use an intermediary, make sure that there is nothing in any documentation which gives anyone other than yourself control of the copyright or of the copies of the book which are produced.

There are two snags involved in self-publishing. The first is the matter of storage, which will not concern you if you have a reasonably large house, but might be a problem in a small flat. Books take up an awful lot of room. The second problem is much more serious and is summed up in the word 'distribution'. How will you reach the maximum market for your book? It will probably be easy enough to tell your relatives and friends about it, but if you have any hope of getting your investment back, and if you want a wider readership than your intimates can provide, then you need to be able to distribute the book throughout the land, and perhaps even abroad. There is no easy answer to this problem. Advertisements can bring some sales (remember to add a charge for postage and packing), and will certainly do so if you can insert an ad in a magazine targeted at a readership which is likely to know you and be interested in what you have to say, but the cost may be substantial; leaflets may also be effective, especially again if inserted in a magazine which goes to people who are likely to want to read your story, but you have to pay for them to be printed and for the insertion in the magazine, and if, instead of distributing them through a magazine, you rely on the mails, the cost of postage can be horrendous.

What you really need is to get the book into bookshops.

This may not be too difficult in your immediate neighbourhood. Most bookshops (at least, those which are independent and therefore don't need to have head office approval) are willing to take copies of a book by a local author and put them on display, although they will normally take them only on sale or return, which means of course that they won't pay you anything unless they sell the books. And they will certainly want a discount; if you are a friend, the discount might, as a special favour, be as low as 25%, but even if you are a regular customer it is more likely to be 33⅓% or 35%. Don't be surprised if the bookseller asks for an even bigger cut – W.H. Smith demands 48% off the cover price of local authors' books. The big problem comes outside your immediate neighbourhood because you will probably not be willing or able to travel the length and breadth of the country visiting bookshops and persuading them to take copies, and even by correspondence the task would be laborious in the extreme and quite expensive.

Distribution has always been the killer for self-publishers, and it is one of the main reasons why Author–Publisher Enterprise was set up. It is an organization which exists to help and support self-publishers, and can offer advice and information. It may not solve your distribution problems, but it will certainly be worth your while to make contact, which you can do at Author-Publisher Enterprise, 7 Kingsland Road, West Mersea, Essex CO5 8RB (tel: 01206 382558).

Although it would be gratifying to see your book on sale throughout Britain and also overseas, in the end I'm afraid that you probably have to resign yourself to a market which is limited to areas which you can service yourself without too much trouble and expense. That is no reason for not going ahead, but simply for making sure that you do not print any more copies than you can be sure of selling.

One thing which you can do and which may eventually

turn out to be more profitable than you might think is to write to the Chief Librarians of the various counties, suggesting that they should buy copies of the book. If they refuse, then you could offer to present copies, and few will turn down such a suggestion in these days when library budgets are constantly being cut. The value for you in getting the book into libraries, even if you have to give it for free, is not only that you will probably achieve a wider readership, but that you will be able to register the book for Public Lending Right (see Chapter 8).

Yet another possibility is to duplicate a few copies only – say, half a dozen – for private circulation among your relatives and friends. If you have a word processor, you can easily run them off; if not, a typescript can be photo copied quite cheaply. You can then take the copies in the form of loose pages to a local firm (Yellow Pages again) which will bind them for you. Or you could put them in ring binders. In Chapter 7 I suggested that you should never use that form of binding, but I was referring then to preparing a typescript for submission to a publisher. Editors don't like typescripts which are in solid, heavy lumps, but your friends and relatives may be quite prepared to accept your book in that sort of format.

Vanity Publishing

It is important to distinguish between self-publishing, subsidy publishing and vanity publishing. Self-publishing may indicate that the author is vain, and often does, but it is not at all the same as vanity publishing. The term is, in fact, a technical one, applied to a certain kind of publishing arrangement. A typical vanity publisher works like this:

1. Advertisements asking for submissions are placed

under headlines reading 'Authors Wanted' or 'Books Wanted' or 'Want to Get Published?'. These ads are give-aways – no regular publishers need to ask for submissions, their problem being more how to cope with the vast numbers that they receive anyway.

2. When an author submits a typescript, the vanity publishers reply promptly saying that the book is splendid, that they want to publish it, and inviting the author to come to their offices.

3. At the interview, the vanity publishers explain that, because publishing conditions are so difficult, they will need a small subsidy from the author towards the production costs. The amount of the subsidy depends on their assessment of the author's wealth, but will always cover the entire costs of production, plus the vanity publishers' profit. It will probably be at least £5,000, and will more likely reach £8–10,000. (This differs from the case of an author offering a subsidy to a regular publisher, because that subsidy will cover only a part of the actual production costs and will be returnable as soon as profits allow.)

4. The vanity publishers then tell the author that he or she will soon recoup the subsidy, because he or she will be paid a royalty of 33⅓ per cent, whereas the normal royalty on a hardcover book would be 10 per cent. However, no royalties will be payable on the first 400 copies printed, which will be used as review copies, for publicity purposes, and for the author's copies, which he or she will be able to purchase, usually at the full retail price (regular publishers allow authors to buy copies of their books at a discount). Since the vanity publishers will not print more than 400 copies of the book, it is clear that the author will never get a penny back.

5. The vanity publishers will also talk of their team of representatives who will market the book in every book-shop in the country, and of the efforts they will make in

sending copies to every newspaper and magazine in which a review might appear. Alas, all the bookshops know the vanity publishers and will not stock the book, and equally, and for the same reasons, the book will get no attention at all in the national press.

6. The vanity publishers' contracts are always meticulously drawn up and are watertight legal documents. They commit themselves to nothing in writing which they do not do, and even their oral promises are carefully hedged so that even if the author has secretly tape-recorded the conversation, there is nothing in it to give a basis for legal action against the vanity publishers concerned.

Is there nothing good to be said about vanity publishers? Well, the production is usually excellent. If you have a book to publish, a few thousand pounds for which you have no other use, and you want the book to appear in a an impressive style, then by all means go to a vanity publisher. But remember that you will not get any of your money back, and the only people who will read the book are those to whom you give the copies which you will have to buy. It's much cheaper and more satisfactory in every way to self-publish instead.

Citron Press

A halfway house between regular publishers and the vanity variety has recently emerged in the form of the Citron Press. If you submit your book to them it has to be accompanied by a cheque for £399.95 (that being the figure at the time of writing). Your book will not be automatically accepted, as it would be with a vanity house, but will be editorially assessed. If the firm does not think the material is of a high enough standard, the typescript and your money will be returned. If Citron decide to publish, they will retain the money, but will produce your book in paperback format, market it, and pay you a 7½ per cent royalty on all sales. The books, which are sold primarily through the Citron Press bookclub, retail at £5.99 (again using current figures), so you would need to achieve sales of about 900 copies to get your money back, but although that may sound like quite a small quantity, not all books will reach the target figure.

Citron Press is a new venture, launched in August 1998. It appears to have achieved an initial success, and if it continues on that path will undoubtedly have its imitators. In a few years' time, there may be a number of such outlets for new authors, including those who can produce a well-written and interesting autobiography. But do be cautious, and make sure that any firm which offers this kind of service will behave ethically.

Selling Part of Your Work

One other possibility to be considered if you fail to interest a publisher in your book is that you may be able to sell extracts from it to a newspaper or magazine. The material would have to be of general interest for a newspaper to take it (although a local rag might be attracted simply because you reside in the area it covers), and an article should probably not run to more than 500 to 1,000 words. A magazine is more likely to be willing to publish you if the article you submit is particularly aimed at the specialist field which it covers itself, and it might be prepared to take something of greater length, or indeed a series of articles. If you sell work in this fashion, you will grant the newspaper or magazine First British Serial Rights (see Chapter 8), but will retain your copyright.

Finally

Remember that publication is not everything. Writing the book will give you great pleasure – at least I hope so – and if even after you have finished you do nothing more with it, it will still be there as an achievement. You will perhaps have learned something about yourself, you will probably have got things off your chest, you may have put some message across. Above all, it will be a record, and as the years go by, it will become more and more fascinating – both to your contemporaries and to those who come after you.

Index